TUTTA PASTA

Tutta

PASTA

LINDY WILDSMITH

Lindy Wildsmith

AURUM PRESS

For Jonathan and Sophie

First published 1994 by Aurum Press Limited,
25 Bedford Avenue, London WC1B 3AT
Copyright © 1994 by Lindy Wildsmith

A catalogue record for this book is available from the British Library.

ISBN 1 85410 294 X

10 9 8 7 6 5 4 3 2 1
1998   1997   1996   1995   1994

Illustrations and design by Don Macpherson
Cover photograph by Peter Letts
Typeset by York House Typographic Ltd
Printed in Great Britain by Hartnolls Ltd, Bodmin

CONTENTS

PASTA E FORMAGGIO
Parmesan plus *91*

PASTA PARTICOLARE
Party pasta *97*

INTRODUCTION

In 1969 I set off for Italy to learn Italian. Then as now, most foreign students went to Florence, but I went to Bologna. Well known throughout Italy for its university and its food, *Bologna la dotta e la grassa* (literally 'Bologna cultured and well-fed') is bypassed by the millions of tourists who visit Italy.

Yet Bologna is an elegant and welcoming medieval city. Her richly coloured sandstone façades glow like embers against the deep blue night sky. Her porticoed buildings give shelter from the rain, protection from the piercing cold and shade from the blistering heat. Her university, the oldest in Europe, nestles under two cock-eyed twelfth-century towers that cast their shadows over some of the finest restaurants and shops in the country. Her pedestrians and her palaces must have been the first to be protected from the motor car by the creation of a traffic-free centre, affording the visitor perfect peace in which to explore the historic town. Muffled footfalls, voices and laughter echoing along the arches and galleries and the toll of an occasional church bell replaced the screech of brakes, the roar of the engine and the crunch of gears more than twenty years ago.

Bologna became my home for a year. The flat where I lived was small and had two bedrooms. One I shared with Luisa; the other was occupied by il Signor and la Signora Monetti together with a highly polished and very large 'Napoleonic' bedroom suite, a remnant of a much grander lifestyle. The rest of the flat consisted of just one small room, with a pantry-sized kitchen at one end screened off by a floral curtain. At the other end stood a sideboard which contained plates for at least a dozen guests, and a single ample armchair. The rest of the room was filled by a glass-topped table large enough to seat twelve people.

La Signora Monetti was an elegantly rotund lady with steel-grey hair and bright blue eyes, kind, intelligent, endlessly patient and a genius in the kitchen. It is to her that I am indebted for the speed with which I mastered Italian and for introducing me to Italian food as very few people have the privilege. I was fascinated by the wonderful stuffings and pasta dishes, by the unusual vegetables cooked, not in water as they were at home, but in milk and butter and cheese and tomatoes and *pancetta* and sometimes even deep-fried in a light batter. I had never seen a raw chicken boned and stuffed and sewn up again, or pieces of veal rolled up with Parma ham around slivers of parmesan cheese, fixed with cocktail sticks to resemble little birds, or savoury rolls made of tender beef, eggs and spinach. La

1

Signora Monetti produced all these in the course of an average week.

Once I had been shown around and introduced to all the tradespeople I was encouraged to do the shopping and became well known in the *quartiere*. I enjoyed running errands because it gave me a chance to show off my Italian and to chat with the convivial and gregarious characters on both sides of the counters. I loved visiting the greengrocer, the butcher, the baker and most of all the *alimentare*, a true Aladdin's cave of cheeses, hams and salamis stacked and hung from floor to ceiling.

During those first months every word and taste was new. Certainly my most fluent Italian was on the subject of food. I used to sit transfixed at la Signora Monetti's enormous glass table (protected at one end by a huge board) and watch the food being prepared, making notes and asking questions. Luisa and I were allowed to grate the parmesan cheese, beat the eggs to bind the meat stuffings, make the breadcrumbs for the cutlets and even to make the *pastella* for the *fritti*, but all the major culinary tasks were carried out by la Signora herself. This was my apprenticeship.

The Monetti home was small but the welcome it afforded was vast. On high days and holidays friends and family alike were invited to share our feasts and it was not uncommon for the huge table to be full. La Signora Monetti made a *sfoglia* (home-made egg pasta) as regularly as my mother made shortcrust pastry. She was such an expert that it neither took very long nor looked very difficult. Her hands and forearms were strong and sinewy; I can see them now pounding the dough until it was like silk to the touch and then rolling it this way and that, stretching it around the rolling pin until it formed a large transparent sheet.

The *sfoglia* was generally used for tagliatelle which were served with a variety of sauces: the traditional creamy meat sauce known as *ragù*, cream and mushroom sauce or *la pommarola*, a fresh tomato sauce. Often at weekends the *sfoglia* was used for lasagne but for very special occasions la Signora Monetti always made tortellini. The stuffing, a delicate mixture of pork fillet, turkey breast, ham, mortadella, parmesan cheese, and nutmeg was prepared the day before and allowed to rest.

Next day, out would come the *matterello*, the metre-long rolling pin and the huge pastry-board which had to accommodate it. Out came the flour and the eggs, and off she would go, kneading, rolling, and cutting the *sfoglia* into squares. Then it was a case of all hands on deck, to stuff, fold and roll the tiny rings of pasta. This is a craft that requires agile fingers. Luisa had been folding tortellini since she was a child; I had not, and it took time before mine could be used. When the tortellini were ready they had to be laid out to dry. The flat was so small that bathing had to be postponed for 24 hours while the tortellini lay in state on boards across the bath.

During my first year in Italy I seized the opportunity to visit as many places as possible. Modena, Milan and Mantua, Venice, Verona and Vicenza, Parma, Padua and Pisa, Florence, Ferrara and Faenza, Ravenna and Reggio are all within easy reach of Bologna, each of these a town with its own history and identity, its distinctive architecture, its people, dialect and *la cucina*.

When I went to Rome for the first time (a monumental step in the eyes of my Bolognese friends, who thought Rome was the beginning of the end of the civilized world), I felt as if I had arrived in another country. I was over-charged by a station porter, fell out with a taxi-driver, was dismayed to discover nothing familiar on the hotel menu and felt utterly deflated at having to enlist the help of a waiter I could barely understand to find me something to eat. My spirits eventually rose when I realized my predica-ment had nothing to do with being a foreigner. I was Bolognese: I spoke with a Bolognese accent and I had acquired a Bolognese way of thinking. As such I could not be expected to be familiar with Rome, the Romans or their food. I was soon to be beguiled, though, and the time would come when my Bolognese friends stared in disbelief at my Roman ways.

Food is seasonal in Italy. The summers are long and hot and most fruit and vegetables grow abundantly. Italy has no need to import expensive, tasteless produce out of season. The street markets in the centre of all the big cities are full of very fresh food brought in daily from the countryside. I used to live in Campo dei Fiori in the heart of old Rome, where every working day, winter and summer, the cafés open to warm the street porters and traders with coffee and brandy as they go about the business of setting up their stalls. Huge, white umbrellas give shelter to everything from flowers to a vast tuna fish rising, opened mouthed, from the centre of a staggering array of fish so fresh that it fills the surrounding air with the scent of the seaside, to stacks of cheap pots and pans, kitchen utensils and earthenware dishes. There are stalls selling every conceivable type of herb, vegetable, fruit, fresh and cured meat, poultry, game, cheese and fish – providing, of course, that they are in season.

Good food is universal in Italy. There are, of course, elegant restaurants in fashionable places where entrance is limited to those who can afford to pay; but there are many more restaurants packed with all kinds of people simply because the food is good. Italians eat out regularly and expect excellence. The waiters have to work hard and yet do their job with style and pride and good humour. Food is cooked to order and is always fresh.

There is no greater diversion than spending a relaxing hour over an aperitif in one of the well known street cafés and watching the beautiful world go by. In every city, however small, on every fashionable street (and every city has one), at certain times of the day you will find girls and boys, men and women of all ages *a passeggio* – sauntering, talking, laughing, arguing and gesticulating.

When you have finished your aperitif and the stage starts to empty, and the pangs of hunger are stronger than the desire to be amused, turn off the well-known roads and squares into the quiet, narrow back-streets and

3

little-known spaces. Here you will findplenty of places to eat. Do not be put off by small restaurants tucked into gloomy and quiet corners; if the restaurant is busy it will be good. Don't take too much notice of the menu; look at the food on show and at what other people are eating. If the waiter speaks English, or you Italian, ask his advice. You will be in for some fabulous surprises and the local waiters will be delighted to find that you, too, like good food.

To start, why not try some pasta . . . *buon appetito!*

THE BASICS

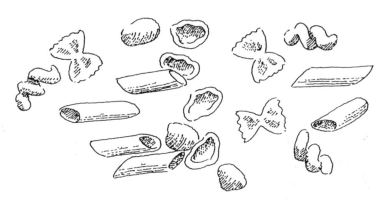

READY-MADE PASTA

There is much speculation about the origin of maccheroni, as the first known pasta was called. For a long time it was supposed that Marco Polo brought it back from China. Then a will was found, dated twelve years prior to his return from the Orient, in which maccheroni is mentioned. It is now supposed to have been introduced to Sicily by the Arabs during the Moorish occupation. From there it passed to Genoa and Naples which, like Palermo, had the perfect climate for drying pasta before the advent of the mechanized drier. The Neapolitans, however, claim it as their own invention. They swear to this day that there is no sunshine, no water and no grain the world over to match theirs and that they alone can produce perfect spaghetti.

All manufactured pasta is made with semolina flour ground from durum wheat. It can be divided into two categories. The first includes spaghetti, bucatini, pasta shapes, shells, tubes and so on, which are all made from semolina flour and water. The second, *pasta all'uovo*, is made from semolina flour and eggs and is used to make tagliatelle, lasagne, cannelloni, etc.

Pasta made with semolina flour is uniquely translucent, has a wonderful waxy golden colour and is richer in protein than home-made egg pasta made with regular baking flour. Durum wheat used to make semolina flour grows in the south of Italy on sunny, rough terrain, whereas 'tender' wheat grows on the plains of the north. Hence the tradition for *pasta all'uovo* in the north and pasta made from durum wheat in the south.

Today the manufacture of *pasta secca* (dried pasta) in Italy is big business, a highly mechanized and computerized industry. The quality of the flour is so important that the major pasta producers mill their own. The durum wheat enters the plant whole, is ground, mixed with water or eggs, kneaded, then rolled and cut or extruded into shape in one continuous process. One producer alone, the second largest in Europe, manufactures 3,750,000 servings of pasta daily, or 63,000 tons a year!

The whole process is charted in a computer room that would not be out of place at NASA. A lone technician watches the schematic progress of the product around the factory. Once in a while he moves out of his glass box into the mill to perform the task that has remained unaltered since milling began: he bends down, scoops up a handful of flour, smells it and tastes it to test its quality.

The importance of pasta to the Italian cannot be overstated. He yearns for it when on foreign soil. There is even a national museum of spaghetti in Rome. It was created by the Agnesi family, who have collected fascinating paintings, illustrations, literature, documents, photographs, machinery, utensils, serving-dishes and pots and pans pertaining to the making and eating of spaghetti since it first became popular.

SHOPPING, STORING AND MAKING LIFE EASY

Producing delicious authentic pasta dishes does not depend on fresh pasta. Many Italians use dried pasta all the time, reserving freshly made egg pasta, either home-made or shop-made, for special occasions. It is easy to pick up 'fresh' chilled pasta from a local supermarket or delicatessen but I prefer to use good-quality dried pasta. Very occasionally I make my own for a *rotolo ripieno* (pasta roll – see page 109), *tagliatelle al boragine* (tagliatelle flavoured with borage), *pansooti di magro* (ravioli filled with white fish – see page 31) or some other speciality that is not available ready made. It is worth buying the 'fresh' tortelloni or tortellini, as the stuffings in the dried ones have a rather harsh flavour and it is a tremendous labour of love to make your own.

When buying pasta, look for Italian brand names such as Agnesi from Imperia, Arriga from Turin, Barilla and Braibanti (inventors of the first fully mechanized pasta plant in 1933) from Parma, Delverde from Abruzzo and Buitoni from Milan. The old established firms produce the best. There are stringent laws in Italy governing the pasta industry, so the quality is guaranteed. There are more than six hundred manufactured pasta shapes, and often the same shape is sold under different names by different manufacturers. The choice of shape is very much a question of taste – what is important is the sauce you serve with it. I hardly dare say it, but meat sauce should never be served with spaghetti!

Even now, with vast supermarkets in every town, it is sometimes difficult to find the pasta you want. They all stock a large range of shapes, but whereas their own brands are always available they constantly change the Italian ones, so that a favourite brand may become suddenly unavailable.

When I came back from Bologna twenty years ago it was very difficult to find the right products to cook authentic Italian food. Elizabeth David's book, *Italian Food*, was my bible: her recipes produce excellent results, using readily available ingredients. I used to make pilgrimages to Italian stores to buy good-quality Italian pasta products, maize flour for polenta, Italian oval-grained rice for risottos, Parma ham, fresh parmesan cheese, good quality salamis, creamy mozzarella cheeses steeped in trays of whey, baskets of fresh ricotta cheese, and fresh basil and pine nuts for pesto sauce. Luckily most of these things are no longer difficult to find, though for such delicacies as pecorino cheese and mozzarella *di bufala* (made with buffalo milk), you may still have to scour an Italian shop. There are large Italian communities in most major cities, with the inevitable *alimentare* selling all that is dear to the Italian *a tavola*. Where there are no Italian grocers, major stores and high-class delicatessens generally stock a good selection of Italian products.

Excellent pre-packed long-life mozzarella, ricotta and mascarpone are now easy to come by. One particular brand, Polenghi, is so good it could almost be the real thing. For anyone living outside major cities, these open up a whole spectrum of deliciously light and refreshing pasta sauces flavoured with spices or fresh herbs. They are good in salads and make unusual puddings as well.

Ready-grated parmesan cheese, whether sold loose or in packets, has a strong, smelly-feet sort of taste, and a sawdusty texture, guaranteed to ruin the flavour of the best sauce. Avoid it at all costs. Fresh parmesan cheese may seem expensive, but 200 g (½ lb) will go a very long way and will keep almost indefinitely if wrapped well in the refrigerator. The fine powdery effect of grated parmesan is obtained by using the lemon zester side of the grater. Never throw away the rind as it gives a lovely flavour to the stock-pot.

When buying salamis, mortadella, Parma ham and fresh parmesan cheese, watch how they are cut. A quarter-pound (100 g) of Parma ham will make a delicious starter for six people if sliced paper thin and served with melon or fresh figs, but if it is sliced like cooked ham it will hardly feed two people and will be hard and unappetizing. There is nothing more frustrating or uneconomical than a piece of parmesan cheese which is either all rind or has been cut so thinly that it disintegrates into little pieces too small to grate. In Italy neat pieces of parmesan, with a small proportion of rind, are persuaded off the cheese with a chisel-like tool rather than cut with a wire or knife.

I try to keep a selection of pasta in the house: at least two packs of fine spaghetti (not the quick-cook variety) and two packets of some type of tagliatelle, one pack of penne and one pack of rigatoni or other similar shape. Cans of tuna, sardines, artichoke hearts, anchovy fillets, baby clams and plum tomatoes are useful. Add a bottle of good olive oil and an assortment of herbs and spices, a few onions, some garlic, parmesan cheese, eggs, bacon and butter and I can magic a dozen simple pasta dishes without having to go shopping first. With some long-life mozzarella, mascarpone or ricotta in the fridge and a packet of smoked salmon pieces or mixed seafood in the freezer, I can create an elegant pasta feast to flatter unexpected guests whatever their taste, and still have time to enjoy their company.

I make double quantities of pasta sauces that require a lot of preparation, then freeze half so that there is always something available for a family meal if I do not have time to prepare one. I also freeze small quantities of left-over roast meat, cooked ham, casseroles and so on, to make into a pasta sauce when needed. Do not freeze cooked pasta.

We do not grow vegetables in our garden, but we do have a small herb garden under the kitchen window, where I grow dill, bronze and green fennel, tarragon, oregano, marjoram, thyme, sage, rosemary, borage, mint, savory, bay, chives, garlic, and sometimes parsley and coriander. I use them all in my pasta sauces. Unfortunately basil, one of the most important Italian herbs, is very delicate and difficult to grow outdoors in cooler climates. Most nurseries and some supermarkets sell potted basil in early summer, and it is well worth keeping a plant on your kitchen windowsill – it will last late into the autumn if you keep picking it.

The flavours of dried and fresh herbs are quite different, and they need to be used in different ways. Dried herbs are fine for heavy, wintry dishes that undergo long cooking processes; fresh herbs can stand alone as an addition to a simple cream, butter or tomato sauce and alter the flavour dramatically. They also make a pretty garnish, especially when in flower.

COOKING AND SERVING PERFECT PASTA

In the introduction to the Penguin edition of her book, *Italian Food*, first published in 1963, Elizabeth David notes: 'In our big towns new Italian restaurants open monthly. . . . Scarcely a week passes but somebody writes an article in a national paper or magazine extolling the glories and subtleties of Italian cooking. . . . Every year appear new cookery books giving more or less accurate versions of the best Italian recipes.' This was never more true than in the nineties, and yet we are still eating plates of stodgy spaghetti smothered with strong-tasting, sloppy tomato sauces and sprinkled with stale, packaged parmesan cheese and calling it Italian. Needless to say, there are restaurants where you can be sure of pasta cooked to perfection and dressed in subtle and interesting sauces.

The great Artusi, father of contemporary Italian cooking, wrote at the turn of the century that pasta should be cooked *al dente*, which literally means 'to the tooth' or 'biteable', because it tastes better and is more easily digested. The cooking time printed on the back of the packet, as a confirmed Italian bachelor once pointed out to me, is accurate – it can take anything from 5 to 15 minutes depending on the type of pasta; fresh pasta takes only a few minutes. Start tasting it a couple of minutes before the suggested time is up, so as to catch it just at the right moment. It is better slightly undercooked than overcooked: overcooked pasta loses its flavour and texture.

Pasta has not always been cooked like this. In the fifteenth and sixteenth centuries, when flour was much coarser, it was boiled for two hours, not in water but in chicken or meat broth and, on holy days when meat was forbidden, in salted water enriched with butter. Sometimes it was cooked in sweetened almond milk or even goat's milk, strained and then flavoured with butter, cheese and spices. I can only imagine that it tasted more like a milk pudding than pasta. By the end of the sixteenth century the cooking time had already been drastically reduced to half an hour.

To cook a 500 g (about 1 lb) pack of pasta you need 5 litres (9 pints) of water and a good handful of coarse salt. (You will need a very large pan.) Bring the water and the salt to the boil and pour in the pasta. If cooking spaghetti, do not break it up: hold it in your hand as you would a bunch of flowers, lower it into the middle of the pan and let it go, allowing it to fan out around the edge and gradually immerse itself in the boiling water. Make sure the water comes back to the boil as quickly as possible. Stir well and continue to stir at regular intervals to ensure that it does not stick. Keep a rolling boil going all the time and do not wander off while the pasta is cooking.

When the pasta is cooked *al dente*, remove the pan from the heat and strain it thoroughly through a colander, keeping back about 2 tablespoons of the pasta water to 'dress' the pasta. Pour the pasta, water and the sauce into a very large bowl and mix well, turning it over and over as you would a salad. Sprinkle with parmesan, chopped herbs, fried breadcrumbs or chopped nuts depending on the recipe and serve at once.

The pasta may be poured back into the hot pan and dressed there if you are using a sauce that is awkward to mix, or one that requires extra heat, to melt cheese, for example. Do make sure that you cook the pasta for a little less time if using this method as it will carry on cooking in the warmth of the pan.

The Italians never warm plates or dishes, as this can cause the pasta to go stodgy and the sauce to dry out. I usually keep the dishes near the cooker while the pasta is cooking so that they are not stone cold.

I have already mentioned that different types of pasta call for different types of *condimento* (sauce). Rich béchamel sauces and ragùs made from minced meats, kidney, chicken liver or game are best served with the wider tagliatelle or pappardelle made from egg pasta, or short fat grooved shapes such as rigatoni. A simple tomato sauce suits small pasta shapes such as farfalle (butterflies or bows) and thin spaghetti or bucatini. Sauces made with olive oil and garlic, with or without tomato or seafood, go well with spaghetti. Sauces made with cream and butter taste best served with small shapes and thinly cut tagliatelle, tagliolini and trenette. Finally, sauces with a raw egg base are excellent served with either spaghetti or short, smooth pasta tubes such as penne (quills).

Pasta is complemented by the addition of freshly grated cheese, which need not be parmesan. Pecorino, caciocavallo, gruyère and fontina all make excellent additions and are used traditionally in different regions of Italy. Grated cheese should not be served with fish sauces, with the one exception of squid with spaghetti. I also like to serve grated parmesan with delicate cream-based fish sauces.

I have recently seen, in certain restaurants, huge rough pieces of parmesan, glistening as if just separated from their parent cheese, brought to the table and grated directly on to the pasta with a well-worn, tarnished grater. You can serve it this way at home, but if this is too messy you can grate a small amount into a dish before you sit at the table, as the Italians do. Alternatively, buy a special parmesan cheese holder-cum-grater that looks like a double pepper-mill. A small piece of parmesan cheese fits inside and each person grinds the amount they want directly on to their pasta. The cheese comes out coarser than is traditional, but it is a handy if extravagant gadget for the family table.

Away from Italy pasta is usually treated as a main course. If serving it as a starter, cook a light main course to follow, unless you have some good trenchermen coming to eat! A banquet-style Italian meal consists of an *antipasto* like prosciutto and figs or *crostini* (slices of French bread topped with savouries and baked in a hot oven) or a selection of salamis. Then comes the pasta, followed by a fish course. Next come the meat and vegetables, then the cheese, and lastly the pudding or fresh fruit.

Rather than eating a heavy meat course with rice, potatoes or bread, the Italian fills up on pasta, and follows with a little meat and salad. In some regions of Italy it is not uncommon to be served pasta tossed in the pan juices of the roast meat or game that is to follow. The meat is then served 'dry' with a few vegetables. Italian dishes are rich and succulent, not 'saucy'.

Pasta itself is considered an excellent ingredient for a healthy diet: low in fat and salt, it provides iron, protein and fibre and is very filling. Over the past five years, pasta sales in this country have risen 10 per cent every year, although our average consumption of 1 kg per person per year is nothing compared to that of the average Italian, who eats 26 kg a year!

Many of the recipes in this book feature butter, cream, cheese and meat, but for the health-conscious there are many others using olive oil, vegetables and fish. Toasted breadcrumbs, chopped herbs or ground nuts can be used instead of grated parmesan cheese.

Some of the best evenings are spent sitting round a table with friends. Eating out is a splendid way of getting together because everyone is relaxed and no one has to worry about the food, but it is becoming ever more expensive and the food is often disappointing. Cooking a pasta meal is an excellent alternative. Many of my sauces are made from ingredients in the storecupboard and prepared in the time it takes to cook the pasta. You can lay the table, make a salad and open the wine while waiting for the water to boil. Without any effort you have an informal meal; add a few flowers, a couple of candles, some cheese and fruit and you have a romantic feast. I love cooking but I do not enjoy spending all day in the kitchen before a party. By choosing food that is quick and easy to prepare or that can be made in advance, I am able to enjoy the cooking *and* the meal.

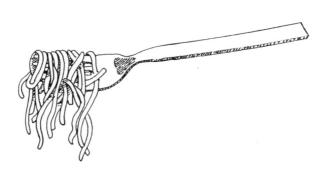

ABOUT THE RECIPES

Each recipe is graded according to the time and effort involved in its preparation:

- * the sauce can be made from start to finish in little more time than it takes to cook the pasta
- ** the recipe is quite time-consuming
- *** the recipe is complicated, or involves home-made pasta

- ✱ the sauce can be made in bulk and frozen or stored in the refrigerator in a screw-top jar under a film of olive oil
- ● the sauce is made entirely from basic ingredients found in a well stocked kitchen

Conversion

1 lb is not the exact equivalent of 400 g but it is the nearest round figure, which to my mind makes weighing much simpler. Consequently if you follow the metric quantities you will have slightly less than the imperial measures.

Quantities

Most of the pasta recipes in this book include 400 g (1 lb) of standard pasta or 250 g (10 oz) of egg pasta. As a rough guide, these quantities will give four average servings for a main course or eight servings for a starter. However, it very much depends on what else is being served. If you are eating a starter and pudding as well as a pasta main course, 400 g may feed six or eight people.

Ready-made fresh pasta

Fresh pasta expands less than dried pasta when it is cooked. 400 g (1 lb) of standard pasta is roughly equivalent to 600 g (1½ lb) of fresh pasta; 250 g (10 oz) of dried egg pasta is equivalent to 375 g (1 lb) of fresh egg pasta.

Left-over pasta

Pasta can be successfully and quickly reheated in a microwave if closely covered with cling film.

THE ESSENTIAL RECIPES

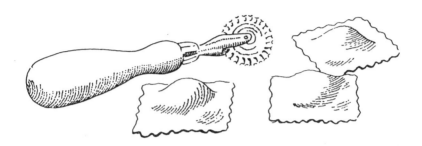

HOME-MADE PASTA

Fresh pasta is generally made from plain flour and fresh eggs and is sometimes flavoured and coloured: green by adding spinach, borage, or other young greens and herbs; red by adding tomato; pink by adding beetroot; black by adding squid ink. For the health conscious, wholemeal and buckwheat flour can also be used.

There are three distinct types of fresh pasta. The first, *pasta fatta in casa*, is the good, old-fashioned, home-made pasta which not so very long ago every Italian housewife prided herself on. The second, *pasta artigianale*, is produced on a small scale in a *pastificio*, like bread in a local bakery. In Italy these *pastifici* are found in most residential shopping areas. This type of pasta is a good compromise: it is made using a mixture of plain flour and the semolina flour normally used in factory-made pasta, and eggs. It is sold fresh and bought by the kilo, piled onto cardboard trays and tied into little paper parcels. Outside Italy, *produzione artigianale* is rare and only found in big cities where there is a large Italian community. The third type, pre-packed 'fresh pasta', is sold by major supermarket chains and speciality shops from chilled cabinets.

All three types are used to make tagliatelle or fettuccine, as they are sometimes called, tagliolini, trenette, and pappardelle; pasta rectangles for lasagne, cannelloni and fazzoletti; flat shapes such as farfalle and maltagliati; and stuffed pastas like ravioli, tortellini and tortelloni.

We eat pasta very regularly at home and I find a good quality Italian factory-made egg pasta is just as palatable if not more so than a mediocre 'fresh pasta'. Buitoni does a range of excellent egg pasta called Rasagnole which comes in various widths and has something of the texture of old-

13

fashioned, home-made pasta. It's worth shopping around for brands such as Agnesi, Braibanti and Delverde, which are very popular in Italy.

There are many regional variations of home-made pasta. In Liguria, for example, egg and water or sometimes water and a little white wine are used to mix the pasta. In Puglia a mixture of semolina and baking flour is used which is bound only with water. Home-made egg pasta is traditional all over the north of Italy; since the Bolognese are generally considered the originators, and as I served my 'apprenticeship' in a Bolognese kitchen, it is their method that I follow.

All you need to make a good *sfoglia* are fresh eggs, plain flour and, to begin with, a great deal of patience. It is not difficult but it takes practice and if you do not follow the 'golden rules' set out below it can go disastrously wrong.

I must have seen a *sfoglia* being prepared a hundred times while I lived in Bologna, but when I was finally allowed to have a go, my pasta ended up as *quadrettini* (little squares) in broth. I was put off making my own pasta for a long time, but then I was presented with a traditional *matterello* (a long Italian pasta rolling pin) encased in a special linen bag tailor-made to match my kitchen. This trophy I was told had belonged to la Signora Monetti's sister or possibly to la Signora herself. I felt that I could no longer make excuses and that I should really make the effort and practise.

You can of course do the whole thing by machine: simply knead the flour and eggs in a processor or electric mixer and put the dough through one of the many pasta machines that are on the market. It requires a lot less skill, and many would say that it is just as good. However, for those of you who would like to have a go at making a *sfoglia* and who are not particularly machine-minded, here is the traditional method passed on by generations of Bolognese cooks to la Signora Monetti, who used it for 70 years, and who has now passed it on to her daughters and granddaughters and to me.

The Golden Rules

1. Never beat the eggs before adding them to the flour.

2. Always use your hands to mix the eggs into the flour.

3. Make sure the kitchen is cool before you start and remains at an even temperature; a sudden draught caused by an open window or door can make the pasta too dry and cause it to crack.

4. Try to use free-range eggs as the yolks are generally much darker and give the pasta a good rich colour.

5. Be precise when measuring out ingredients: use 100 g (or exact imperial equivalent, 3½ oz) flour to 1 size 2 egg.

Pasta all'uovo
(Home-made egg pasta)

300 g (10½ oz) plain flour
3 medium-sized eggs

Sieve the flour onto a flat surface (either a large board or table-top) to form a volcano shape. Make a well (*fontana*) in the centre of the flour large enough to accommodate the eggs. Break the eggs one at a time into a cup and pour them into the well.

Now very carefully (and holding your hand straight) work the egg into the flour with the tips of your fingers, taking care not to allow the egg to escape.

Knead the dough for 15 to 30 minutes, depending on your expertise, until small air bubbles appear on the surface and the dough has a dry silky texture, like a firm scone dough. It should spring back into shape when pinched.

If you are a novice divide the dough into three equal balls. Wrap two of them in a dampish tea towel and set to one side, and repeat the following instructions for each piece of dough:

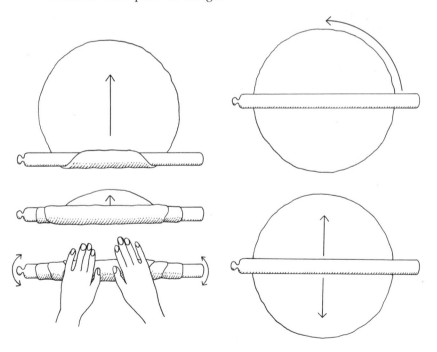

Make the pasta into a ball and then flatten it with the palms of your hands. Take a rolling pin, preferably a long one, and begin to roll the dough out as evenly as possible retaining its round shape. When the *sfoglia* resembles thin pastry, sprinkle it with flour and roll it around the rolling pin, then roll it on itself with your hands flat across the top of the pin. Use plenty of flour to ensure that it does not stick to itself.

Unwind the *sfoglia*. Give it a quarter turn anticlockwise, roll flat and repeat the process until the sheet is really thin, round and even. Roll it a little bit more; it should be paper-thin and transparent and handle like a piece of fabric. If you are working on a wooden board you should be able to see the grain through the pasta.

Leave the pasta sheet to dry, covered with a clean tea towel, while you roll out the other pieces of dough.

Do not attempt to roll out a *sfoglia* with a pastry rolling pin with handles as you will never get it thin enough or large enough or smooth enough, even if you have cut it into three pieces. Most good cook shops sell a straight wooden rolling pin about 50 cm (20 in) long, which should suffice. The larger the rolling pin, the larger the *sfoglia*, the larger the *sfoglia* the longer the tagliatelle; the longer the tagliatelle the smaller your bills! At least this is what they say of a good Bolognese housewife – *conti corti e tagliatelle lunghe!*

Roll each sheet of pasta up as you would a piece of paper and cut it into strips with a good sharp knife. Pappardelle should be 2 cm (¾ in) wide, tagliatelle 1 cm (⅜ in), trenette 3 mm (⅛ in) and tagliolini as thin as you can possibly cut them.

For lasagne and fazzoletti cut the *sfoglia* while still flat into pieces 12–15 cm (5–6 in) square or 10 cm (4 in) square for cannelloni. For farfalle or strichetti (bows) cut the *sfoglia* with a serrated pastry wheel into strips 2 cm (¾ in) wide and then cut these again every 4 cm (1½ in). Squeeze these little rectangles in the middle to gather up the pasta until it sticks.

Green Pasta for Lasagne Verdi

300 g (10½ oz) plain flour
300 g (12 oz) spinach
2 eggs

Wash the spinach thoroughly in running water and then put it into a large pan with just the water that is left on the leaves and a little salt. Simmer until tender. Strain off the water by pressing the spinach in a colander and then leave it to cool.

Squeeze the spinach between the flats of your hands until it is quite dry. If you do not do this the pasta will be much too wet and will be impossible to roll. Chop the spinach very finely on a board with a sharp knife or *mezzaluna*, or press it through a sieve.

Sieve the flour onto a work surface or table-top, making a volcano-shaped pile, and make a well in the middle large enough to take the eggs and the spinach purée.

Put the spinach and the whole eggs into the well and very carefully, holding your hand straight and using only the tips of your fingers, work the spinach and eggs into the flour. Now knead the dough with as much strength as you can muster. If it is at all sticky add more flour until the dough is dry but soft. Keep kneading until small air bubbles appear on the surface and the dough is silky to the touch.

Roll the dough according to the instructions for *pasta all'uovo*. Leave the *sfoglia* to dry a little before cutting it into tagliatelle 1 cm (⅜ in) wide or lasagne 12–15 cm (5–6 in) square.

SWEET AND FRAGRANT GNOCCHI

These were the words used by an eighteenth-century Italian poet to describe these tiny, irresistible dumplings. They are made with mashed potato, semolina, maize flour or ricotta and sometimes flavoured with puréed spinach, minced chicken, ham and even mint. So numerous are the ways of making gnocchi and so numerous the regions that have adopted them that I have decided to include a small section on this delightful pasta family.

There are many ways of serving gnocchi: plain and simple with the addition of butter and parmesan, with pesto as they do in Genoa, with a meat sauce as in Bologna, a mushroom sauce as in Tuscany, a *matriciana* sauce as in Rome or with black butter, a pinch of cinnamon and a pinch of icing sugar as is traditional in Venice. In Friuli they use a mixture of smoked ricotta, candied peel, cocoa, sultanas and icing sugar which I confess I have not got around to!

Gnocchi di patate
(Potato gnocchi)

This recipe for gnocchi was given to me by Tina Monetti in Bologna. They are not difficult to make, just time-consuming, but well worth the effort. These quantities will make enough for four hungry people as a main course or eight as a starter.

1 kg (2½ lb) potatoes
600 g (1½ lb) plain flour

Boil in salted water or steam the potatoes in their skins until tender, peel them and put them through a potato ricer or sieve until they are quite smooth.

Add the flour a little at a time until it is all mixed in and the dough no longer sticks to your hands. Knead well.

Flour the work surface. Break off lumps of dough and roll them into long sausage shapes 1½ cm (½ in) thick. When all the mixture is used up cut them into pellets about 2 cm (1 in) long.

With the thumb, lightly roll each pellet along the back of a fork or fine grater to form a shell-like shape with a pattern on the outside.

Bring a large pan of salted water to the boil. Drop in the gnocchi a few at a time, taking care not to cook too many at once as they will stick together. Cook for 2–3 minutes, or until tender, and remove with a slotted spoon a few at a time as they come to the surface.

Serve simply with melted butter and parmesan or meat, tomato, mushroom or pesto sauce.

Gnocchi verdi
(Green gnocchi)

1 kg (2½ lb) potatoes	1 egg, beaten
400 g (1 lb) spinach	salt and nutmeg to taste
300 g (¾ lb) flour	

Boil the spinach in very little salted water until tender. Drain thoroughly and chop very finely. When it has cooled squeeze out any remaining water with your hands.

Boil or steam the potatoes in their skins until tender, peel them, and put them through a potato ricer or sieve until quite smooth.

Mix in the flour, spinach, salt, egg and a grating of nutmeg and proceed as for *Gnocchi di patate*.

Gnocchi di pollo
(Chicken gnocchi)

Other poultry or cooked ham may be used to flavour these gnocchi.

200 g (8 oz) potatoes	2 egg yolks, beaten
100 g (4 oz) chicken breast	30–40 g (1–2 oz) flour
50 g (2 oz) grated parmesan	salt and nutmeg to taste

Boil or steam the potatoes in their skins until tender. Peel them and put them through a potato ricer or sieve until quite smooth.

Meanwhile steam or lightly boil the chicken breast and mince very finely.

Mix the potatoes, chicken, parmesan cheese, flour, beaten egg yolks, salt and a grinding of nutmeg and proceed as for the basic recipe. Cook for 2 or 3 minutes and serve with melted butter.

Gnocchi al forno con formaggio
(Baked gnocchi with cheese)

1 quantity of chicken gnocchi	emmenthal cheese
150 g (6 oz) fontina or	50 g (2 oz) butter, cut into slivers

Preheat the oven to 220°C (425°F, gas 7). Grease an ovenproof dish and cover the bottom with a layer of gnocchi. Cover this with a layer of cheese, and repeat the layers until the gnocchi and cheese have been used up (make sure that the top layer is of cheese). Dot the surface with butter and cover the dish.

Place in the oven for 5 minutes and serve at once.

Gnocchi di semolina
(Semolina gnocchi)

These are commonly known as *gnocchi alla romana* but it is generally accepted that they originated in Piedmont.

500 ml (1 pint) milk	*2 egg yolks, beaten*
100–150 g (4–6 oz) semolina	*salt and nutmeg to taste*
50 g (2 oz) grated parmesan	*100 g (4 oz) melted butter*

Heat the milk in a heavy-based pan until it starts to simmer. Add the semolina a little at a time and stir it in until the mixture is thick enough to support a spoon. This amount can vary according to the quality of the semolina. Beat hard to ensure there are no lumps and cook for 20 minutes.

Remove from the heat and add 1 tablespoon of parmesan cheese, the beaten egg yolks, a pinch of salt and a grating of nutmeg. Mix well.

Butter a couple of baking trays. Pour enough mixture onto each tray to make a layer ½ cm (¼ in) thick. Level out with a wet palette knife and leave to cool. When it is quite cold cut the sheets of dough into discs 2–3 cm (1 in) in diameter.

Preheat the oven to 200°C (400°F, gas 6).

Grease an ovenproof dish. Starting with the off-cuts, layer the gnocchi in the dish, brushing each layer with melted butter. Overlap the discs and work round the dish in decreasing circles, until you end up with a sugar loaf effect.

Pour over any remaining butter, sprinkle with grated parmesan and brown in the oven for 10 minutes or so.

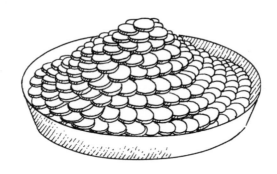

Gnocchi di ricotta

(Ricotta and spinach balls)

This Tuscan recipe is from Anna Gosetti della Salda's book *Le ricette regionali italiane*. Gnocchi di ricotta are traditionally cooked and served in broth but I prefer to serve them in a sauce.

400 g (1 lb) spinach	*3 tbs freshly grated parmesan*
300 g (¾ lb) ricotta or	*cheese*
300 g (¾ lb) cottage cheese sieved	*salt and nutmeg to taste*
with 3 tbs double cream	*a little flour*
3 eggs, beaten	

Wash the spinach well and cook it with just the water left on the leaves. Strain and allow it to cool. Squeeze the spinach to remove any remaining water. Chop finely and sieve into a bowl.

Add the ricotta, eggs, parmesan cheese, salt and a grating of nutmeg to the spinach and beat well. Add enough flour to make the mixture easy to handle and beat again.

Form the gnocchi by taking a teaspoon of the mixture at a time and rolling it into a ball between the palms of your hands.

Meanwhile bring a large pan of salted water to the boil. Pour in the gnocchi and cook for 3 or 4 minutes.

Drain them and transfer to a large serving bowl. Add either butter or a tomato sauce, sprinkle with parmesan cheese and serve at once.

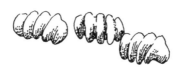

GOLDEN POLENTA

Polenta in one form or another has been the national dish in Italy since prehistoric times. The Romans were nicknamed *pulmentari* or *polentoni* because of the quantity of polenta they ate, made not from maize but from spelt wheat or mashed vegetables. Polenta made from barley, millet or buckwheat flour was the staple food of peasants in northern Italy for centuries.

It was not until the sixteenth century, when maize was introduced, that polenta as we know it evolved. It has an acquired, frugal taste, and for me a little goes a long way. It does have its devotees and recently, being *di moda*, has found its way on to some elevated menus.

Left-over polenta can be cut into finger-sized pieces, split in two, filled with stracchino cheese and then fried in oil. The frugality completely dissolves into the rich creamy filling and the crunchy outer coating! *Polenta pasticciata* is characteristic of most northern regions. It is cut into slices and layered in an earthenware dish with plenty of butter and cheese and sometimes with the addition of a rich sauce made from sausage, giblets or meat. It is then placed in the oven until brown and bubbling – an excellent winter dish.

Polenta can be served with the rich meat, game and fish sauces in this book.

400 g (1 lb) coarse yellow maize
flour (or fine polenta flour)
1400 ml (2¾ pints) water (or
1300 ml (2½ pints) if using fine
polenta flour)
1 tsp salt
75 g (3 oz) butter

Bring the salted water to the boil in a large pan, pour in the flour and beat quickly, making sure that no lumps form. Reduce the heat and cook very slowly for 50 minutes, stirring regularly. (This may seem like an excessive amount of time but polenta should be well cooked.) Just before it is ready add the butter and stir well.

Place a clean, damp tea towel over a large chopping board and turn out the polenta in a single mass. Cut it into slices a centimetre thick using a length of fine string, like a cheese wire.

Serve at once while piping hot with the sauce of your choice.

22

USEFUL SAUCES
Béchamel sauce

Used in many pasta dishes, especially oven cooked pasta. Like other basic sauces, cheeses, herbs, spices, meat and fish can be added to it to ring the changes.

50 g (2 oz) butter   *500 ml (1 pint) warm milk*
50 g (2 oz) flour   *salt and nutmeg*

Melt the butter, add the flour and cook gently. Add the warmed milk gradually. Cook over a low heat stirring constantly with a small wire whisk until the mixture is smooth and thick.
Add a little salt to taste and a grinding of nutmeg.

Panna liquida
(Cream)

Cream is used as the base for many pasta dishes and is particularly suited to egg pasta, whether factory- or home-made. All kinds of meat, fish and vegetables can be added to this sauce, flavoured with fresh herbs and spices. The pasta should be coated, not swimming, in the sauce.

For anyone who prefers to avoid cream, a mild bio yoghurt makes an excellent substitute, but care must be taken when heating it lest it should curdle.

For 250 g (10 oz) egg pasta

250 ml (½ pint) single cream   *a grinding of black pepper or*
25 g (1 oz) butter   *nutmeg*
2 tbs parmesan cheese

Combine the ingredients and warm through over a gentle heat. An excellent accompaniment for all types of stuffed pasta.

Sugo di pomodoro
(Simple tomato sauce) * ● *

I learnt to make this simple and subtle tomato sauce in Campania. It forms the basis of many pasta dishes, particularly those using shellfish and vegetables. It is one of the simplest sauces I know and one of the most versatile. Artusi recommends its use because of its taste and its health-giving properties. He says it even settles stomach upsets!

800 g (2 lb) canned plum
tomatoes, drained and deseeded
reserved tomato juice
4 tbs olive oil
a few stems of fresh basil,

oregano or other fresh herbs
2 whole cloves of garlic
small piece of fresh chilli (optional)
salt and pepper to taste

Place the tomatoes, olive oil, herbs, garlic, chilli (if using), salt and pepper in a heavy-based pan and simmer for 30 minutes until the tomatoes have become thick and creamy. Mash from time to time. (It may be necessary to add a little of the reserved tomato juice should the sauce start to dry out.) Discard the garlic clove and chilli before serving.

Condimento di pomodoro

(Tomato sauce) * ● *

This is one of la Signora Monetti's recipes. It is used for dressing stuffed home-made pasta, spaghetti and tagliatelle, and as a basis for many meat dishes and soups. It has a *battuto* of chopped celery, carrot and onion as its base which gives it a stronger flavour than the *sugo di pomodoro*.

1 small stick of celery
1 small carrot
1 small onion
10 fresh basil leaves or other
fresh herbs
400 g (1 lb) fresh plum tomatoes

or 800 g (2 lb) tinned tomatoes,
drained and deseeded
reserved tomato juice
25 g (1 oz) butter and 2 tbs
olive oil
salt and pepper to taste

Chop the celery, carrot, onion and herbs very finely with a *mezzaluna* or sharp knife. Gently heat the olive oil and butter in a heavy-based pan. Add the tomatoes, chopped vegetables and herbs, salt and pepper. Cover the pan and cook over a very low heat for 1 hour. Stir from time to time and add a little of the reserved tomato juice if the sauce starts to stick.

When the sauce is thick and creamy put it through a sieve and use as required.

This sauce will keep in a screw-top jar under a film of olive oil in the refrigerator.

La conserva di pomodoro

(Signora Colombini's tomato conserve) ** *

Signora Colombini, a Neapolitan by birth, was a regular visitor to the Monetti household in Bologna, and gave me this recipe. It is an excellent way of using up tomatoes at the end of the summer. Diluted with a little butter, water or cream and with the addition of a few fresh herbs, home-made *conserva* makes an excellent accompaniment to pasta and meat dishes through the winter. It can also be used as the base for tomato soup.

5 kg (12½ lb) ripe plum or round
tomatoes
2 carrots, finely chopped

2 sticks of celery, finely chopped
1 very large onion, finely chopped
salt to taste

Wash the tomatoes, cut them into quarters and place in a large pan with the chopped vegetables and salt. Cook, covered, over a low heat for an hour or until the vegetables are soft. Now pour the mixture into a colander lined with a clean, white tea towel and allow the vegetables to drain for 2 or 3 hours. Discard the juice and sieve the tomato mixture to remove the skins and seeds.

Put the purée into small pots, and seal them tightly. Place the pots in a large pan of water and boil for an hour.

This conserve will keep for 12 months or more. As each jar is used cover what is left with a little olive oil and it will keep in the refrigerator for up to two weeks.

PASTA CLASSICA

A selection of regional recipes

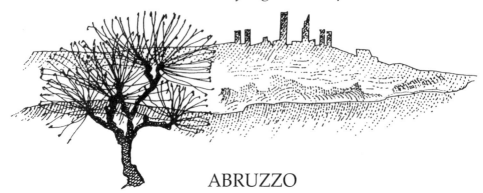

ABRUZZO

Abruzzo is the mountainous region of Italy that lies to the east of Rome, running along the Adriatic coast. Its long, snowy winters have given rise to all kinds of deliciously warming specialities, known to everyone who has spent a skiing holiday there.

Red chilli peppers appear in all kinds of unexpected dishes, and are known not as *peperoncini*, as they are commonly called in Italy, but very aptly as *diavolini* (little devils). The famous *spaghetti all'arrabbiata*, made with chilli, olive oil, parsley and garlic, was invented here.

A meal in the Abruzzese mountains should finish with a tot of the local liqueur, *centerbe*, enjoyed by the side of a roaring fire. It is made, as its name suggests, with a hundred or more herbs gathered in the area, but it is no flowery potion. Every sip courses like fire through the veins, slamming the door once and for all on the freezing weather outside.

Spaghetti o penne all'arrabbiata
(Spaghetti or quills with chilli) * ●

This is a simple and delicious dish, but it must have plenty of bite. *Arrabbiata* means rabid and is used metaphorically in Italian to mean angry. The dish should be made quickly by pouring the best quality, smoking hot olive oil, flavoured with garlic and chilli over the thinnest spaghetti, cooked *al dente* and served at once. Follow these rules and you will love it; if you do not it will be stodgy and dreary. The dish can be made in 10 minutes from start to finish.

Garlic lovers can replace the chilli with extra garlic and again, if made correctly, the result is sublime.

400 g (1 lb) thin spaghetti or pasta
quills
150 ml (6 fl oz) good olive oil

2 cloves of garlic, chopped
1 chilli pepper, chopped
a handful of parsley, chopped

Bring a large pan of salted water to the boil. Pour in the pasta and cook *al dente*.

While it is cooking, heat the olive oil gently and add the garlic and chilli. When the garlic turns golden brown remove it and the chilli from the pan and discard them both.

Strain the pasta and transfer to a large serving dish. Add the boiling hot oil and the chopped parsley, stir well and serve at once.

Trenette al ragù d'agnello

(Trenette with lamb and pepper ragù) ** ✳

A ragù of lamb pieces and peppers is traditionally served with *maccheroni alla chitarra*. I have modified the recipe to use my favourite combination of fennel seeds, peppers and lamb, which I first discovered in a leafy courtyard at Cervetri, after visiting the famous Etruscan tombs nearby. Like all meat sauces, this benefits from standing overnight; it also freezes well.

400 g (1 lb) trenette or thin
tagliatelle
3 tbs olive oil
400 g (1 lb) minced lamb
1 glass of red wine
1 clove of garlic, crushed
½ tbs fennel seeds

a little lemon juice
4 yellow or red peppers
400 g (1 lb) tinned tomatoes,
strained and deseeded
reserved tomato juice
salt and pepper to taste
grated pecorino cheese

Heat the olive oil, add the minced lamb as soon as the oil is hot and fry for 10 or 15 minutes or until browned.

Reduce the heat and add the red wine, crushed garlic, fennel seeds and a squeeze of lemon juice and cook until the liquid has evaporated.

Remove the stalks and seeds from the peppers, and slice them very thinly. Add the peppers and tomatoes to the meat, season with salt and pepper to taste, cover the pan and cook for 1½ hours over a low heat. Add a little of the tomato juice if the sauce dries out.

Towards the end of the cooking time, bring a large pan of salted water to the boil. Pour in the pasta and cook *al dente*.

Strain the pasta and transfer to a large serving dish. Add the sauce, the pecorino cheese and 2 tablespoons of pasta water. Stir well and serve at once.

LIGURIA

Liguria stretches in a rainbow arc from the French border, along the Italian Riviera and down to Tuscany. Its magnificent coastal road winds the length of the region, never straying far from the azure calm of the Mediterranean, through elegant resorts and stunning countryside.

The Riviera cook, known for being 'careful', makes the most of the produce that abounds in this land of eternal summer. Ligurian food is based on *aromi naturali*, natural seasonings and little or no animal fat. Wild herbs, vegetables, nuts and olive oil are used to dress the pasta. Ravioli are filled with greens, herbs and fish. The spongy pizzas are covered with a tomato and onion sauce, olives, whole garlic, anchovy and basil. Pies are filled with vegetables and rice.

Lie on the beach in the morning when the Liguri are taking the sun or walk through the shady streets in the late afternoon when they are *a spasso* and above all you hear talk of food, of recipes and all sorts of other culinary chatter.

Trenette al pesto genovese
(Trenette with pesto) * *

In an eighteenth century history of the Genoan people, trenette al pesto was recorded as the traditional festive family dish. This marked an important development in the history of Italian pasta, as up until the seventeenth century it was flavoured simply by adding either cheese, sweet spices, honey, sugar, cinnamon or butter: there were no sauces as such. Maccheroni with tomato sauce, a Neapolitan invention, was not recorded until 1830 and meat and fish sauces evolved after that.

Pesto is made from basil, toasted pine nuts and pecorino cheese and is the pride of the Italian Riviera. The basil grown in the fields in summer and under glass out of season is sold in fragrant posies in every greengrocer's the length of the region. Pesto's delicate flavour is perfect with any kind of pasta but trenette and spaghettini are most favoured. Pesto can also be added to minestrone soup and salad dressings to give them an extra special flavour. Traditionally it is prepared with a pestle and mortar but it can be made quickly and simply in an electric blender.

This particular recipe was given to me by a warm and enthusiastic Ligurian who cooks in his spare time in his daughter's restaurant and who went to great lengths to tell me about the local specialities. He recommends adding a spot of butter to the pesto to preserve the colour. The half walnut is his little vanity: whether you use it is up to you – I do!

400 g (1 lb) trenette
36 basil leaves
1 tbs pecorino and 1 tbs parmesan
(or 2 tbs parmesan)
a fistful of toasted pine nuts,
roughly chopped
1 small clove of garlic,

roughly chopped
a tiny pinch of salt
a tiny knob of butter
half a fresh walnut, roughly
chopped
half wine glass of olive oil

Put the basil leaves in a blender and chop. Add the other dry ingredients and grind until smooth, then add enough olive oil to bind. Pour into a screw-top jar, cover with a film of olive oil and store in the refrigerator until required.

Bring a large pan of salted water to the boil. Pour in the pasta and cook *al dente*.

Place 3 tablespoons of pesto and 2 of pasta water in a large dish and mix. Strain the pasta, add it to the pesto and mix thoroughly, adding a touch more pasta water if the pesto does not stir in smoothly. Serve at once with more parmesan.

Bagna de carne
(Meat sauce with mushrooms and pine nuts) ** *

When I was offered spaghettini with meat sauce I was mutely horrified. Meat sauce and spaghetti are not generally served together in Italy. But as was quickly pointed out, I was not in Italy – I was in Liguria! This is not the rich ragù of the Bolognesi but the *sugo* of the Liguri. As you will see, meat sauce it may be by name but hardly by nature!

The sauce is served traditionally with trenette or ravioli made with plain or green egg pasta. In other parts of Italy spinach is used to colour and flavour green pasta, but here beet leaves, borage and other herbs are used instead. The pasta made with beet leaves is darker in colour and more solid in consistency than pasta made with spinach, and it has a very distinctive flavour.

400 g (1 lb) pasta	in milk (optional)
1 onion	400 g (1 lb) tinned tomatoes,
3 tbs olive oil	strained, deseeded and chopped
100 g (4 oz) minced meat	rosemary and thyme
25 g (1 oz) pine nuts	salt and pepper
a few dried mushrooms, soaked	

Chop the onion very finely and soften in olive oil until transparent.

Add the meat and a little salt and fry until browned. Then add the pine nuts, mushrooms, tomatoes and herbs and cook over a low heat for an hour, stirring at regular intervals, until dense and creamy.

Cook the pasta of your choice *al dente* in plenty of salted boiling water, strain and mix well with the sauce. Serve with grated parmesan.

Penne mare e monti

(Quills with wild mushrooms and seafood) **

The head waiter of the Panama restaurant in Alassio, where we ate this stupendous dish, hotly denied that it was a local speciality. But to a captivated stranger its name, 'sea and mountain pasta', will always be reminiscent of the stunning scenery and delicious food of the area.

The porcini mushrooms had been gathered that morning in the misty hills which look down on Alassio, a mellow resort of the Riviera dei Fiori. The shellfish had been caught in the calm waters around Gallinera, the bottle-nosed island close to the shore. I have adapted the recipe to use fresh mushrooms and ready-cooked mixed seafood, freely available in large supermarkets.

500 g (1¼ lb) pasta quills	300 g (12 oz) ready-cooked mixed
olive oil	seafood
1 clove of garlic and a handful of	salt and pepper
parsley, finely chopped together	3 large ripe tomatoes
100 g (4 oz) oyster mushrooms	125 ml (¼ pint) mixed single cream
100 g (4 oz) shiitake mushrooms	and pasta water

Cover the base of a large, heavy-based saucepan with olive oil, add the *battuto* (finely chopped parsley and garlic) and the mushrooms. Stir together carefully over a low heat. If you are using fresh uncooked shellfish it should be added at this point (ready-cooked fish should not).

Cover the pan and cook over a very low heat for 15 minutes, stirring from time to time to ensure the mushrooms do not stick. Add salt to taste.

Plunge the tomatoes in boiling water and remove the skins. Cut them in half, discard the seeds and then chop roughly and add to the pan.

Cover again and cook for a further 10 minutes. Stir from time to time until the tomatoes have started to colour the sauce a pale pink.

Then add the ready-cooked seafood, warm the sauce through over a low heat and leave to stand until the pasta is almost ready.

Boil the pasta in plenty of boiling salted water.

When the pasta is almost ready add the cream and an equal quantity of pasta water to the sauce and heat through. Once the pasta is *al dente*, strain and add it to the fish and mushroom sauce. Mix well over a low heat and serve at once, turned out into a large shallow bowl.

Ravioli di magro
(Ravioli filled with fish) ***

There are many traditional ravioli fillings besides this fish one. Mixtures of herbs such as borage, beet leaves, pimpernel, nettles and ground elder are boiled, chopped finely and added to stuffings made of tripe, chicken liver, cocks' combs, giblets, sausage or simply cheese. I use a *sfoglia* made with borage, but spinach or beet leaves can be used instead or you can make a plain egg *sfoglia* (see page 15).

Filling

a handful of parsley	400 g (1 lb) mixed herbs (see
1 small clove of garlic	above) or spinach
400 g (1 lb) white fish	3 eggs
olive oil	25 g (1 oz) grated parmesan
salt and pepper	a grating of nutmeg

Chop the parsley and garlic very finely with a *mezzaluna*. Clean the fish, add the *trito* (the parsley and garlic mix), olive oil, salt and pepper, wrap in greaseproof paper (or tinfoil if using a grill) and leave to marinade for several hours or overnight.

Cook the fish in its parcel, either in the microwave for 4 or 5 minutes or under a medium grill for 8 or 10 minutes, turning the parcel once, until just cooked. Meanwhile cook the greens in salted water, strain and squeeze thoroughly until quite dry.

Skin the fish, carefully remove the bones and flake the flesh lightly with a fork. Then add the fish to the greens and chop finely with a *mezzaluna*, adding salt and pepper to taste.

Beat the eggs and add to the fish mixture with the grated parmesan and a grating of nutmeg. Mix well.

Cover and leave to stand in the refrigerator until required.

The Pasta

50 g (12 oz) young borage leaves
(older leaves are hairy and bitter-tasting)

300 g (10½ oz) plain flour
3 eggs
a touch of water

1 quantity of fresh tomato sauce (see page 23)
freshly grated parmesan cheese

Place the young borage leaves in boiling salted water and boil for 3 minutes until tender. Strain, squeeze thoroughly, chop finely and allow to cool.

Sieve the flour onto a flat surface (either a large board or table-top), forming a volcano shape. Make a well in the centre of the flour large enough to accommodate the eggs and the borage. Mix and roll according to the instructions on page 15.

Divide the pasta into four and roll four separate *sfoglie*. Cover each one with a damp cloth to keep them moist until required.

Place small teaspoonfuls of filling in rows on the first *sfoglia* at 3 cm (1¼ in) intervals until it is completely covered. Then take a second *sfoglia* and lay it on top of the first and press down firmly between the rows to seal the pasta together, thus marking out the ravioli.

Take a fluted pastry wheel and run it down each row, thus cutting the ravioli into 4 or 5 cm (1½ or 2 in) squares. Repeat with the remaining *sfoglie*.

Lay the finished ravioli out on trays lined with a clean, dry teacloth and leave to dry for at least 2 hours.

Cook in small batches for a few minutes, in plenty of salted water, removing the ravioli from the pan with a slotted spoon as they come to the surface. Arrange them carefully on a wide serving dish.

Add a covering of fresh tomato sauce and lots of parmesan cheese.

BOLOGNA AND EMILIA ROMAGNA

Bologna is the regional capital of Emilia Romagna, the large region of Italy that nearly spans the width of the peninsula at the top of the boot, from the Adriatic coast in the east to Liguria in the west. Bologna is special to me because this is where I first discovered the delights of Italy, Italian food and the Italians.

It is a beautiful medieval city renowned for its architecture, university, industry, and food and in particular for home-made pasta in every guise: tortellini, tortelloni, tagliatelle, pasticci, lasagne, rotoli. The whole area is rich in every kind of produce whether farmed or found naturally in its verdant woods and fruitful countryside and the Bolognese know just how to cook and serve their plentiful harvest to perfection.

Tagliatelle al ragù
(Tagliatelle with the classic meat sauce from Bologna) ** *

If you were to ask for *la salsa bolognese* in a Bolognese restaurant I suspect you might be in for a shock! It would be made from dry Marsala wine and oranges, flour, butter and sugar and served with boiled, roast or grilled meat. What is called bolognese sauce by many people is referred to as ragù locally. It has a creamy consistency and is a local speciality served with tagliatelle or rigatoni, but never spaghetti!

This recipe for ragù, along with recipes for *sfoglia*, gnocchi, risotto and many others of la Signora Monetti's specialities are all written down in a tiny grease-spattered notebook which I kept during my first year in Bologna. The ragù freezes very well and can be used for all kinds of pasta dishes such as lasagne, *rotolo ripieno, pasta al forno* etc. It improves if left to stand overnight.

33

400 g (1 lb) tagliatelle
1 small carrot
1 small stick of celery
1 small onion
1 tbs olive oil
50 g (2 oz) butter
400 g (1 lb) lean minced steak
100 g (4 oz) minced bacon

2 tbs white wine
375 ml (¾ pint) milk
1 tbs tomato concentrate
a grating of nutmeg
salt and pepper
2 tbs freshly grated parmesan
cheese
1 tbs chopped parsley

Chop the carrot, celery and onion very finely. Gently heat the oil and 1 oz of butter together in a heavy-based saucepan. Add the chopped vegetables and sweat together until tender.

Add the mince and the bacon, increase the heat and fry until brown. Take care not to burn the vegetables.

Add the white wine, stir and leave to evaporate.

Lower the heat and add enough milk to cover the meat, then add the tomato purée, nutmeg, salt and pepper and stir well. Cover with a lid and continue to cook over a low heat for 1 hour. Stir from time to time, adding a little water if necessary.

Plunge the tagliatelle into plenty of boiling salted water and cook *al dente*. Strain the pasta and transfer to a large serving dish, retaining a small amount of pasta water.

Add the meat sauce, parmesan cheese, remaining butter, and chopped parsley to the pasta with 2 tablespoons of the pasta water and a grinding of black pepper. Mix well and serve at once.

Maccheroni gratinati

(Maccheroni gratin) ✶✶

This is a popular family dish in Italy and makes a pleasant change from lasagne. Tuna, mushroom, chicken, chicken liver and other sauces can be used instead of the meat sauce.

400 g (1 lb) maccheroni rigati or
other pasta
1 quantity of béchamel sauce
(see page 23)
1 quantity of meat sauce

(see above)
25 g (1 oz) parmesan cheese, cut
into splinters
toasted breadcrumbs
salt and pepper to taste

Prepare the meat and béchamel sauces.

34

Preheat the oven to 230°C (450°F, gas 8).

Bring a large pan of salted water to the boil. Pour in the pasta and cook for 2 or 3 minutes less than is usual (the pasta will carry on cooking in the oven).

Strain the pasta and return it to the pan with 2 tablespoons of pasta water and the meat sauce. Mix well and pour it into a shallow, buttered ovenproof dish.

Pour the béchamel sauce over this and scatter the splinters of parmesan cheese over the top. Cover with a layer of toasted breadcrumbs and cook in the oven for 10 minutes.

Serve at once.

Lasagne verdi alla Bolognese

(Bolognese green lasagne) ** or *** if using home-made lasagne

Lasagne verdi are a Bolognese speciality and this is another of Tina Monetti's recipes – the ultimate in authenticity. I use a good Italian factory-made lasagne and although it involves a little extra work I prefer the variety that needs boiling first as the end result is better. A serving of lasagne should be rich and moist, not sloppy. It should be cut out of the tin into squares that keep their shape when put on a plate. The proportion of pasta should be greater than that of the sauces.

a 2-egg sfoglia verde (see page 16) cut into lasagne or 300 g (12 oz) ready-made lasagne
1 quantity of meat sauce (see page 33)

1 quantity béchamel sauce (see page 23)
plenty of freshly grated parmesan cheese
butter

Preheat the oven to 180°C (350°F, gas 4).

Bring a large pan of salted water to the boil. Add 4 or 5 sheets of pasta to the water and boil according to the instructions on the packet. Remove with a slotted spoon, plunge into cold water and lay them out on a clean tea towel to dry. Repeat the process until you have enough.

Butter the inside of a square roasting tin. Cover the bottom with sheets of lasagna laid edge to edge. Cover this sparingly with a thin layer of meat sauce, 2 or 3 tablespoons of béchamel sauce and 1 tablespoon of parmesan cheese. Repeat until all the ingredients have been used up. Finish with a layer of lasagne dotted with butter.

Place in a hot oven for 30 minutes and serve at once.

The top layer should be on the crunchy side.

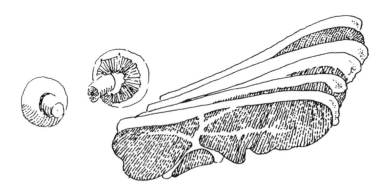

Penne con fegatini di pollo, pancetta e funghi
(Quills with chicken liver, bacon and mushrooms) ** *

Chicken livers are served traditionally in a risotto rather than with pasta, but I like them with pasta. This is a splendid supper dish. The sauce can be made beforehand, set on one side and reheated when you are ready to use it.

400 g (1 lb) pasta quills	*salt and pepper*
100 g (4 oz) chicken livers	*a small glass of red wine*
100 g (4 oz) mushrooms	*milk*
100 g (4 oz) streaky bacon	*tomato purée*
1 clove of garlic	*parmesan cheese*
a few sprigs of fresh tarragon	

Wash and dry the chicken livers. Chop the chicken livers, mushrooms and bacon into small pieces, keeping them separate. Finely chop together the garlic and tarragon.

Gently heat a heavy-based frying pan, add the chopped bacon and fry until the fat runs. There should now be enough bacon fat in the pan to cook the other ingredients – if not add a little olive oil.

Add the chicken livers, mushrooms, garlic and chopped tarragon to the bacon with a little black pepper. Add salt if necessary and cook over a low heat for 5 minutes.

Increase the heat, add the wine and cook until evaporated. Next add a wine glass of milk and a teaspoon of tomato purée to the pan, then cover and cook over a low heat for another 10 or 15 minutes or until thick and creamy.

Bring a large pan of salted water to the boil. Pour in the pasta and cook *al dente*.

Strain the pasta and transfer to a large serving dish, add the chicken liver sauce and 4 tablespoons of grated parmesan cheese. Stir well and serve at once.

Cannelloni farciti di ricotta, parmigiano e aragosta
(Cannelloni with ricotta, parmesan cheese and lobster) **

Filling

300 g (12 oz) ricotta or 250 g (10 oz) cottage cheese and 4 tbs of cream sieved together	1 egg, beaten
	4 tbs breadcrumbs
3 tbs freshly grated parmesan cheese	100 g (4 oz) finely-chopped lobster
	1 tbs chopped fresh thyme*

Put all the ingredients in a bowl and mix well.

* Note: crab can be combined with thyme, salmon with dill and chicken with tarragon to give a range of differently-flavoured cannelloni.

Making the Cannelloni

400 g (1 lb) cannelloni tubes or lasagne	(see page 23)
	50 g (2 oz) grated parmesan cheese
1 quantity of béchamel sauce	25 g (1 oz) butter

Preheat the oven to 220°C (425°F, gas 7).

Bring a large pan of salted water to the boil. Add the pasta and cook until slightly undercooked (the pasta will carry on cooking in the oven). Strain the pasta and plunge it into cold water. Strain it again and dry it by laying it out carefully on a clean tea towel.

If you are using pasta tubes you will need to load a forcing bag with the stuffing and pipe in the filling. If you use lasagne, cut each rectangle into two squares and place a tablespoon of stuffing in the middle of each one, then roll the pasta up to form a tube.

Pile the cannelloni into a buttered ovenproof dish, cover each layer with béchamel sauce and sprinkle with parmesan cheese. Dot with butter and place in the over for 10 to 20 minutes or until brown.

Tortellini alla Bolognese
(Venus knots) ***

There are certain dishes that cannot be made without a freshly made *sfoglia* (see page 15) and although some of them are available ready made (tortellini for example can be bought in most supermarkets) the flavour of the filling cannot compare with the subtle taste of the real thing. Tortellini (pielets) are small squares of pasta filled with meat and then twisted around the fingers to form tiny ring-shaped parcels. They are a Bolognese speciality and are also known as cappelletti (hatlets) and agnolini. There is a delightful legend attached to the tortellino:

Once upon a time, while travelling through Italy, Venus found herself in Bologna. She was exhausted after a very tiring day and called at an inn. The landlord recognised her immediately and gave her his very best room and lavished every attention upon her.

He was captivated by her beauty and could not get her out of his mind. When everybody in the inn had gone to bed and he was sure that they were all fast asleep he decided to take a secret look at his heavenly guest. He took a lamp, slowly stole up the creaking wooden stairs and quietly pushed open the door. There before him lay Venus asleep in all her naked splendour. Never before had the innkeeper seen such perfection. He silently closed the door again and returned to the kitchen.

As he worked into the night preparing the food for the following day his thoughts kept returning to the vision he had seen. Then as he prepared the stuffing for the pheasant and the *sfoglia* for the following day he had a wonderful idea. He worked swiftly and enthusiastically, cutting squares of pasta and filling them with the stuffing, folding them and twisting them around his fingers until he had made dozens of perfect little navels exactly like Venus's: and this is how the tortellino was invented!

Stuffing

150 g (6 oz) lean pork fillet
80 g (3 oz) turkey breast
50 g (2 oz) cooked ham
50 g (2 oz) mortadella
1 egg

100 g (4 oz) freshly grated
parmesan cheese
nutmeg
salt and pepper

Sfoglia

3 fresh eggs
300 g (10½ oz) plain flour

2 litres (4 pints) rich chicken or
beef consommé

Prepare the stuffing a day ahead and let it rest.

Cook the pork fillet and turkey breast in a little butter for about 10 minutes or until tender. Allow the meat to cool and then mince it together with the ham and mortadella. Mix the meat with the egg, parmesan cheese and nutmeg and add salt and pepper to taste. Cover the bowl and leave the mixture to stand for 24 hours.

The following day make a 3 egg *sfoglia* (see page 15).

Cut the rolled pasta into strips 3 cm (1¼ in) wide, then cut these strips every 3 cm to form lots of little squares. Place a small teaspoonful of the filling in the middle of each square.

Fold each square diagonally to form a triangle around the filling. Press the edges together to seal in the stuffing. Now wind the long side of the triangle around your index finger and press the two corners together to form a ring. The third corner should then turn back on itself.

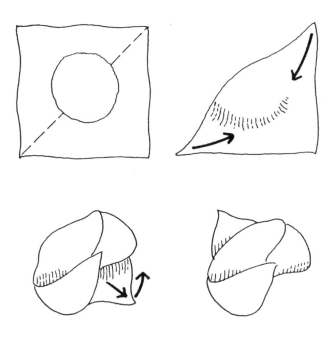

How to fold a tortellino

Alternatively you can cut lots of circles out of the pasta with a small cutter 3 cm (1¼ in) in diameter. Place a little of the filling in the middle of each one and simply fold the circle in half. Press the edges together well to ensure the stuffing does not escape.

Lay the finished tortellini out neatly on floured cloths, leaving plenty of space around each one. The tortellini should then be left overnight to dry out.

The following day bring a large pan containing 2 litres of rich beef or chicken stock to the boil. Pour the tortellini into the boiling stock, stir carefully and cook for 6 to 10 minutes.

It is traditional to serve tortellini in the broth they have been cooked in as a consommé dish with a sprinkling of freshly grated parmesan on the surface *(tortellini in brodo)* and accompanied by a bottle of good Bolognese Lambrusco wine. Alternatively you can scoop the tortellini out of the broth with a slotted spoon, pile them into a serving dish and pour over them a creamy *panna* sauce (see page 23).

Tortelloni alla Bolognese

(Turtló in Bolognese dialect) ✳✳✳

Tortelloni are another Bolognese speciality, similar to tortellini but larger. They are popular all over Italy, the forms and fillings varying from region to region. They are also known as tortelli, ravioli, agnolotti, pansooti and marubini, depending on where they come from. The fillings are made from a mixture of cheese, chopped vegetables, herbs, poultry or fish.

Filling

300 g (12 oz) ricotta, or 300 g (12 oz) cottage cheese and 3 tbs double cream
3 tbs freshly grated parmesan cheese

1 egg
1 clove of garlic and a handful of parsley, finely chopped together
nutmeg

Sfoglia verde (green egg pasta)

300 g (10½ oz) plain flour
300 g (12 oz) spinach
2 fresh eggs

1 quantity tomato sauce (see page 24)

Sieve the ricotta, or cottage cheese and double cream, into a bowl and add the parmesan cheese, egg, parsley and garlic mixture and nutmeg and beat until smooth.

Make the *sfoglia* (see page 15).

Roll it out and cut it into squares 8 cm by 8 cm (3 in by 3 in). Place a spoonful of the filling in the middle of each square, fold the pasta over and press down the sides to seal it, forming rectangular parcels 8 cm by 4 cm (3 in by 1½ in). Lay them out on a board until you are ready to use them.

Bring a large pan of salted water to the boil and gently slide in the little parcels, one at a time. They will take 2 or 3 minutes to cook and will rise to the surface as they are ready. Remove them with a slotted spoon and place them on a large shallow serving dish. Pour the tomato sauce over the top and sprinkle with grated parmesan.

CAMPANIA

Campania's high craggy coastline cascades with luxuriant greenery. Views of Vesuvius across the Bay of Naples are framed by massive umbrella pines and by clouds of bougainvillaea blooms. There are fascinating towns such as Positano and Ravello, some mounted on lofty rocks that fall vertically to the sea and others set into sheltered coves, and the sea is studded with beautiful islands such as Capri and Ischia.

This is an area rich in culinary tradition. Here are to be found excellent sun-ripened tomatoes, olives and olive oil, exquisite mozzarellas and the traditional caciocavallo cheese. Among its delights are light, crisp pizzas, unrivalled deep-fried seafood and luscious dishes of spaghetti flavoured with oregano, basil, tomatoes and shellfish. Other classic dishes of Campania include *insalata caprese*, a salad of tomato, basil, mozzarella and olive oil, from Capri; *spaghetti alla puttanesca,* made with anchovy, chilli, tomato, olives and capers, from Ischia; and *vermicelli alla carrettiera* from the mainland.

Vermicelli alla carrettiera
(*Vermicelli with onions) * ●

Vermicelli alla carrettiera, in the style of the cart driver, is a traditional country recipe. The pasta is served in a sauce made from onions and olive oil and sprinkled not with parmesan cheese but with fried breadcrumbs.

There are many possible variations on this recipe, so this warming supper dish can be tailor-made to suit family and friends by adding a favourite ingredient such as bacon, tuna fish or mushrooms. With the exception of the bacon the extras should be added after the onion has cooked.

400 g (1 lb) vermicelli (very fine
spaghetti)
1 large onion
2 cloves of garlic
1 handful of parsley

100 g (4 oz) streaky bacon
(optional)
olive oil
oregano
salt and pepper
2 tbs breadcrumbs

Chop the onion, garlic, parsley and bacon together finely. Heat 1 tablespoon of olive oil (3 if not using bacon) and fry the *battuto* over a low heat until transparent. Add a grinding of black pepper and a pinch of oregano. In another pan heat 1 tablespoon of olive oil and fry the breadcrumbs until golden.

Bring a large pan of salted water to the boil. Pour in the pasta and cook *al dente*. Strain the pasta, then return it to the pan, add the fried onion mixture and stir well over a low heat for 2 minutes. Then pour into a serving dish, sprinkle with the fried breadcrumbs and serve at once.

Maccheroni alla Napoletana

(Maccheroni with tomato sauce and caciocavallo cheese) ∗

400 g (1 lb) long maccheroni
napoletani (thick spaghetti with a
hole down the middle)
1 onion
1 tbs olive oil
25 g (1 oz) butter
400 g (1 lb) tin plum tomatoes

(reserve the juice)
a few stems of fresh basil or
oregano
salt and pepper
50 g (2 oz) grated caciocavallo
cheese (or parmesan if unavailable)

Slice the onion.

Gently heat the butter and olive oil, add the onion and fry until transparent. Remove the onion and discard, leaving the juices in the pan. Strain the tomatoes and remove the seeds. Add the tomatoes, basil and salt and pepper to taste to the pan and simmer for half an hour (add a little tomato juice should the sauce dry out).

Bring a large pan of salted water to the boil. Break the maccheroni into short lengths and add to the water. Cook *al dente*.

Strain the pasta and transfer to a large serving dish and add the sauce, 2 tablespoons of pasta water and the grated cheese. Mix well and serve at once.

Spaghetti alla puttanesca

(Spaghetti with tomato, chilli, anchovy and capers) ∗ ●

A literal translation of the Italian for this dish is 'spaghetti in the style of the whores'. Whether it was a popular dish with the ladies of the street, or whether the ladies and the dish had the same bite, I wouldn't like to say! It is one of the classic pasta dishes and it comes originally from Ischia, an island off the coast of Campania, close to Naples.

400 g (1 lb) spaghetti	*1 small tin of anchovy fillets*
2 tbs olive oil	*400 g (1 lb) tinned plum tomatoes,*
1 clove of garlic, peeled but not	*strained, deseeded and chopped*
chopped	*100 g (4 oz) black olives*
1 piece of chilli pepper 1 cm	*50 g (2 oz) capers*
(½ in) square	*salt*

Gently heat together the olive oil, the garlic clove and the piece of chilli in a pan (traditionally this would be made of terracotta).

Remove the garlic as soon as it has changed colour and add the anchovy, tomato, olives and capers and continue to cook over a low heat until the sauce has reduced and darkened in colour (about 20 to 30 minutes). Add salt to taste.

Bring a large pan of salted water to the boil. Pour in the pasta and cook *al dente*.

Strain the pasta and transfer to a large serving dish. Add the sauce, stir well and serve at once.

ROME AND LAZIO

I used to live and work in Rome. Eating out was cheap and the working day long, and consequently we hardly ever ate at home. On hot summer evenings we congregated at the busy *osterie*, found in every corner of *Roma Vecchio*. Local characters, artists, expatriots and *villani* squeezed around rickety tables. The din of customers talking above each other and vying for the attention of the waiters, and a never ending stream of itinerant beggars, black market pedlars, nomadic flower sellers and strolling players touting for business all added to *la confusione*.

Penne alla carbonara

(Quills with cream, egg and bacon) * ●

La Carbonara is a rich creamy coating of raw egg, butter, parmesan cheese, cream and pieces of crispy bacon fried with garlic, served with spaghetti or quills. It is one of my all time favourites, the speciality of every simple restaurant in and around Campo dei Fiori.

One of the eating places I liked best used to be *Da Carolina* in Piazza della Quercia, close to Piazza Farnese. Carolina's restaurant was pretty basic but so popular you had to stand and wait for food. If you did not like it she used to tell you where to go in colourful *Romanaccio* terms! This is her recipe.

400 g (1 lb) pasta quills or	*25 g (1 oz) butter*
spaghetti	*125 ml (¼ pint) cream*
150 g (6 oz) bacon	*3 tbs parmesan or pecorino cheese*
1 clove of garlic, crushed	*salt and pepper*
4 egg yolks and 1 whole egg	

Chop the bacon into small pieces and fry together with the garlic until crispy.

Fork the egg lightly and add a knob of butter, the cream, half the grated parmesan and a grinding of black pepper. Leave it to stand without mixing until the pasta is ready.

Bring a large pan of salted water to the boil. Pour in the pasta and cook *al dente*. Strain the pasta and transfer to a large serving dish. Add the bacon pieces and stir well. Stir the egg mixture lightly, pour it over the pasta, stir again and serve at once. The butter will melt and the egg will cook in the heat of the pasta.

Serve with extra cheese and generous amounts of black pepper.

Spaghetti alla matriciana
(Spaghetti with bacon and tomato sauce) ** ● *

This dish comes originally from the Marche area of Italy but it has become popular in the many inexpensive *trattorie* and *taverni* of Rome. According to tradition it should be served with pecorino cheese but if you cannot find this parmesan will do. It is a popular supper dish with family and friends alike, inexpensive and simple to prepare. The sauce can be prepared in advance and set aside until it is required.

400 g (1 lb) spaghetti	*(reserve the juice)*
150 g (6 oz) streaky bacon	*small piece of chilli (optional)*
1 onion	*black pepper and salt*
400 g (1 lb) tinned plum tomatoes,	*2 tbs grated pecorino or parmesan*
drained and deseeded	*cheese*

Chop the bacon into small pieces, place it in a preheated heavy-based frying pan and cook over a medium heat until the fat starts to run. Slice the onion finely. Add it to the bacon and fry over a low heat until transparent.

Add the tomato to the pan with the chilli and a grinding of black pepper and stir well.

Cover and cook over a very low heat for 45 minutes. Stir frequently during the cooking time to prevent the sauce from sticking. If it dries out, add a little of the tomato juice. When the sauce is cooked, remove the chilli.

Bring a large pan of salted water to the boil. Pour in the pasta and cook *al dente*. Strain the pasta and transfer to a large serving dish. Add the sauce and the pecorino cheese, stir well and serve at once.

VENICE AND THE VENETO

The first time I arrived in Venice it was by sea. Since then, car, train and plane have brought me back, but none of these can rival a water-borne entrance to the siren city. In winter, shrouds of mist dull her gold and vibrant colours, veil her bell towers and domes and hang over her canals, muffling the lapping inky water as it rises out of its narrow confines. Boats emerge from the fog, laden with building bricks, barrows and buckets: *lavori in corso*, work in progress!

The vibrant colours of Venice captured on the canvases of artists like Titian and Giorgione are everywhere, not just in the sumptuous interiors and the ornate façades of the Canale Grande and Piazza San Marco, or in the magnificent feast-day processions. They are in the fish markets, bright with shellfish and a rainbow-coloured catch, the busy vegetable stalls piled with colourful produce, in the tempting displays in restaurant windows, in the jars on the delicatessen's shelf, in the wax-coloured cheeses and the bright copper polenta pan. And they are in the famous risottos, white and green with peas, golden with scampi, black with squid ink, red with tomato and on platters filled with orange lobsters, crabs and prawns.

Bigoli con le seppie

(Spaghetti with squid) ** *

This is one of my favourite spaghetti dishes, traditionally made with cuttlefish. I use fresh squid, which is much easier to buy in this country. The sauce is also delicious served with a little crusty French bread or with rice. In Venice the sauce is made with plenty of squid ink which makes the dish as black and as oily as the canal waters at night. If you find this off-putting, the sac containing the squid ink need not be used; the sauce will then have a burnished colour.

Bigoli is the word given to spaghetti in the Veneto region, which is sometimes dyed black with squid ink. This is one of the few fish sauces that parmesan cheese should be served with.

400 g (1 lb) spaghetti	*a handful of parsley, finely chopped*
400 g (1 lb) squid, small if possible	*a glass of white wine*
2 tbs olive oil	*salt*
1 small onion, finely chopped	*parmesan cheese*
1 clove of garlic, finely chopped	

The flavour of the sauce improves and the squid is tenderized if left to stand for 24 hours after it is prepared.

Clean the squid carefully. Pull the head and tentacles away from the body and the insides will come with them. Cut off the insides and discard. Pull away the 'backbone' from the inside of the body and discard (it resembles a large transparent plastic leaf). Rinse out the body to ensure there is no sand or mucus left inside.

Cut the bodies into rings. If the squid are small, the tentacles and head may be left intact; if large, chop them up. Leave wrapped in a clean towel to dry.

Chop the onion and garlic very finely. Heat the olive oil in a heavy-based pan, add the onion and garlic and cook over a low heat until transparent. Add the parsley (reserving a little for garnish) and squid to the pan and fry for 4 or 5 minutes until the squid is pinkish in colour. Increase the heat, add the wine and cook for a further 2 minutes or so.

Reduce the heat to very low, cover the pan and simmer for 30 minutes until tender. Add a little water if the squid dries out too much.

Bring a large pan of salted water to the boil. Pour in the pasta and cook *al dente*.

Strain the pasta and transfer to a large serving dish. Add the sauce. Stir well, sprinkle with chopped parsley and serve at once with parmesan cheese.

Bigoli con noci e ricotta
(Bigoli with a ricotta and walnut dressing) *

This may sound a very odd combination, but from Roman times until 1700 it was common to serve a mixture of sweet and savoury elements. Honey, butter, cacio (a type of cheese) and sweet spices were the original flavourings; parmesan, sugar and cinnamon came a little later. They were not made into a sauce but simply added to the pasta after it was cooked. The use of walnuts, though traditional, certainly does not date back that far; they were included some time in the eighteenth century.

The dressing can be prepared in the time it takes to cook the pasta. This is an ideal vegetarian dish and makes a delicate starter for a supper party if you know your guests like something out of the ordinary. It is utterly delicious!

400 g (1 lb) bucatini or thin	*50 g (2 oz) butter, softened*
spaghetti	*1 level tsp icing sugar*
200 g (8 oz) ricotta or 150 g	*1 level tsp cinnamon*
(6 oz) cottage cheese sieved with	*3 tbs walnuts, chopped*
4 tbs cream	*salt to taste*

Cream the ricotta, butter, icing sugar and cinnamon with a wooden spoon.

Boil the pasta in plenty of salted water until *al dente*. Strain the pasta and transfer to a large serving dish. Add 3 tablespoons of pasta water, the ricotta mixture, and the walnuts. Mix well and serve at once.

Polenta con funghi di bosco
(Polenta with wild mushrooms) *

The most memorable meal of mushrooms I have ever enjoyed was on the romantic terrace of the Villa Cipriani in the Asolano hills north of Venice. The attentive head waiter recommended a plate of golden polenta served with local wild mushrooms. I can remember even now the exquisite flavour and silken texture of those exotic mushrooms, freshly picked and artfully cooked to adorn the steaming golden polenta. The chef, Signor Mario Piana, assured me that the recipe was the usual one and their perfection was due not to their preparation but to the excellence and uniqueness of the local *finferli* mushrooms.

Here is the recipe, certainly the best way to complement freshly picked mushrooms. The mushrooms can be served by themselves as a starter or as a side dish.

1 quantity of polenta (see page 22)	*a handful of parsley, finely chopped*
300 g (12 oz) freshly picked	*half a wine glass of olive oil*
mushrooms	*a little stock or water*
3 cloves of garlic, finely chopped	*salt and pepper to taste*

Wipe the mushrooms clean and mix together the garlic and parsley. Warm the olive oil over a low heat, add the garlic and parsley and cook until the garlic is transparent. Add the mushrooms to the pan and continue to cook until they have soaked up all the oil and start to soften. Add salt and pepper to taste.

Cover and cook for a further 20 minutes. If necessary add a little warm stock or water to prevent the mushrooms from sticking or drying out. Serve piled on top of a slice of freshly made polenta or with your favourite pasta.

Penne alla trevigiana

(Quills with radicchio and smoked bacon) **

Treviso, a delightful medieval city of the Veneto region, is famous for its radicchio. It is reputed to be the finest in the world, certainly in Italy; so much so that it is preserved in olive oil and sold side by side with such delicacies as artichoke hearts and truffles, and at similar prices, in the classiest delicatessen shops.

Once a rarity outside Italy, radicchio is now available from supermarkets and good greengrocers. Radicchio resembles a small compact lettuce with pinky-red leaves and thick white fleshy veins; its texture is like chicory. It is as popular as lettuce in the Italian salad bowl.

This recipe was given to me by my old friend Antonia Mazzanti, a native of the Veneto region.

400 g (1 lb) pasta quills	*chopped*
300 g (12 oz) radicchio, washed,	*50 g (2 oz) butter*
dried and roughly chopped	*125 ml (¼ pint)*
200 g (8 oz) smoked bacon, finely	*single cream*

Melt the butter, add the radicchio and bacon, cover, and cook over a very low heat for 30 minutes.

Bring a large pan of salted water to the boil. Pour in the pasta and cook *al dente*.

Just before the pasta is ready, add the cream to the radicchio and bacon and warm through.

Strain the pasta and transfer to a large serving dish. Add the sauce, stir well and serve at once.

FLORENCE AND TUSCANY

Florence is no stranger to the tourist, art lover or student of things Italian. The historic centre, the heart of the city, is like a grand Renaissance salon in a magnificent museum. Its impact is immediate. Venture out of the city and the countryside calls to mind the landscape backdrops of Medici portraits and religious paintings.

The proud Florentines pride themselves on their language, their good manners and their food. Traditional dishes include thickly cut pappardelle covered in rich game sauces, thick slices of toasted bread topped with chicken livers and rich bean and vegetable soups. Steaks up to a kilogram in weight are seared on both sides on a red hot charcoal grill; spit roast chicken and suckling pig are stuffed with herbs and spices. All are served perfectly by waiters endowed with the skills and charm of a bygone age.

The idea of eating this kind of food in Florence may seem bizarre to those who have laboured between Piazza Signorile and Piazza del Duomo in the searing heat of an August midday. In winter however, the city can be bitterly cold and there can be few better ways to spend the lunchtime hours of *chiusura* than over a leisurely meal in a welcoming restaurant.

Pappardelle alla lepre

(Pappardelle with hare sauce) ** *

Both hare and rabbit are popular meats in Italy and make excellent casseroles as well as pasta sauces. Hare is wild and consequently only available from August to March, while rabbit is bred for the table and can be bought at any time of the year. A hare must be hung and has a gamey flavour. When I can't get hold of hare for this recipe I use rabbit. Italians cut poultry and game into at least 16 pieces. This way it absorbs more flavour and cooks quicker. Any good butcher will do this for you if you ask.

The quantities given in the following recipe will coat 500 g (1¼ lb) pappardelle, with an equal amount of sauce left over which can be frozen for use on another occasion.

500 g (1¼ lb) pappardelle
1 hare
a small bunch of parsley, very
finely chopped
1 stick of celery, very finely
chopped
1 small carrot, very finely chopped
1 small onion, very finely chopped
50 g (2 oz) bacon

1 cup olive oil
salt and pepper
a glass of red wine
a cup of milk
a little stock
1 bay leaf
a grating of nutmeg
freshly grated parmesan

Clean the hare carefully and cut it into small pieces about 5 cm (2 in) square. Chop the parsley, celery, carrot, onion and bacon together very finely. Heat the oil, add the *battuto* of chopped vegetables and bacon and fry until transparent.

Add the pieces of hare to the fried vegetables and bacon, add salt and freshly ground pepper and fry until the meat has browned all over. Add the wine and cook over a medium heat until it has evaporated. Add the milk, a little stock, the bay leaf and a grating of nutmeg. Cover the pan and cook slowly for 1 hour.

When the hare is cooked, remove the pieces from the sauce, then remove the meat from the bones, chop it up roughly and return it to the saucepan.

Bring a large pan of salted water to the boil. Pour in the pasta and cook *al dente*.

Strain the pasta and transfer to a large serving dish, then add 2 tablespoons of the pasta water, half the hare sauce (the other half can be frozen and used some other time) and 2 tablespoons of grated parmesan. Stir well and serve at once.

La minestra alle cinque 'P'

(Pasta and the five Ps) **

This recipe was passed on to me by Ian and Denise Morris who run the Berkley restaurant, tucked away like a box of delights at the top of a twisting flight of stairs. Ian lived and worked in Florence and has greatly influenced the choice of food Denise cooks in the restaurant. They were making their own delicious pasta and serving it *come si deve* (as it should be) long before it was fashionable.

This dish is served only in the early summer when the young peas arrive in Florence from the surrounding hills. The five Ps are *piselli* (peas), *prezzemolo* (parsley), *pancetta* (belly pork), *pappardelle* and *parmigiano* (parmesan cheese). Peas cooked with ham appear over and over again in Tuscan cooking, either as a vegetable, in a pasta sauce or with meat in casseroles.

400 g (1 lb) pappardelle
1 kg (2 lbs) young peas in their pods, or 200 g (8 oz) frozen peas
1 small onion
150 g (6 oz) pancetta or bacon
a handful of parsley
salt and pepper

a little stock or water
1 tsp icing sugar
25 g (1 oz) butter
375 ml (¾ pint) single cream (optional)
2 tbs freshly grated parmesan

Shell the peas. Cut the onion in half longways. Chop the fat part of the bacon up finely and place in a small pan (terracotta if possible) with the two halves of the onion. Heat gently until the fat starts to run freely.

Add the peas, the remaining bacon chopped into small pieces and the chopped parsley, and stir carefully. Add a little salt, a grinding of black pepper and a little stock or water. Cover and cook until tender. If the peas are young this should only take five minutes or so. Add extra stock from time to time should they take longer. Discard the onion and add the icing sugar.

Bring a large pan of salted water to the boil. Pour in the pasta and cook *al dente*.

Strain the pasta and transfer to a large serving dish. Add 2 tablespoons of pasta water, the butter, the single cream (warmed) if desired, the parmesan and the peas. Stir well and serve at once.

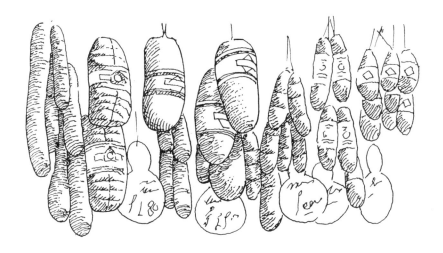

Tagliatelle con salsicce
(Tagliatelle with Florentine sausage) **

This is another of Ian's favourite pasta sauces, a rustic dish he remembers as the prize part of a perfect day spent in the countryside. It was the pride of a country restaurant, made with the simple produce of a Tuscan *podere* (farm): home cured sausages and local olive oil; ripe tomatoes, celery and carrots gathered from the tiny fields that cover the hillsides.

It can be made successfully here too. Good Tuscan olive oil is sold in most delicatessens and tinned plum tomatoes are excellent. Italian sausage is coarse and meaty and no English sausage, however good, can be substituted for it, so use either belly pork or finely chopped Italian salami.

1 medium sized carrot
1 stick of celery
100 g (4 oz) Italian sausage or
belly pork
2 tbs olive oil

400 g (1 lb) tinned plum tomatoes,
drained, deseeded and chopped,
(reserve the juice)
50 g (2 oz) parmesan cheese

Chop the carrot and celery finely together. Chop the sausage finely. Place the meat and vegetables in a pan with the olive oil. Cook over a medium heat until browned.

Add the tomatoes, cover and cook over a low heat for half an hour. Add a little tomato juice from time to time if the sauce dries out.

Bring a large pan of salted water to the boil. Pour in the pasta and cook *al dente*.

Strain the pasta and transfer to a large serving dish. Add the sauce, stir well and serve at once with parmesan cheese.

PUGLIA

Southern Italy was considered wild and barbarous until after the second world war when malaria was finally stamped out and the Autostrada del Sole was built from Milan to the Straits of Messina. Yet it was a land populated by the ancient Greeks long before the rise of Rome and a land where the Normans saw potential for military adventure and established a kingdom which lasted for two centuries.

Puglia is the heel of the famous boot, scenically a land of plenty, possessing some of the most beautiful coastline in the Mediterranean. Its craggy hillsides yield excellent lamb, strong wine and the finest olive oil in Italy. The long hours of sunshine produce a plethora of exquisite fruit and vegetables. The taste of Puglia is of simplicity: home-made pasta shapes, cavatieddi that look like cowrie shells and orecchiette that resemble skull-caps, served with sun-dried tomato and other vegetable sauces. Folded home-made pizze, pasta and lenticchie, bowls of oysters, mussels and clams, paper wrapped fish and grilled lamb are all characteristic of Puglian food. The natural goodness of the produce requires little more than excellent local olive oil as flavouring.

Broccoletti, acciughe e peperoncino con orecchiette
(Broccoli, anchovy and chilli sauce with orecchiette) *

The combination of young tender broccoli and smooth olive oil gives a wonderful creamy texture to this dish and the anchovy, chilli and garlic impart an interesting bite. If you can locate olive oil from Puglia all the better. The taste, fragrance and colour of olive oil alters subtly from region to region and greatly from country to country. Having the right oil for the right dish does make a great deal of difference to its flavour.

This is a simple dressing, one of my favourites. It makes an unusual and utterly delicious starter or main course. It can be made omitting the chilli and garlic without detracting from its excellence.

400 g (1 lb) orecchiette	1 clove of garlic
400 g (1 lb) young tender broccoli	50 g (2 oz) anchovy fillets
a wine glass of olive oil	salt
a piece of chilli pepper	

Bring a large pan of salted water to the boil. Add the pasta and the broccoli and cook *al dente*.

Heat a wine glass of olive oil in a pan. Add to it a piece of chilli (to taste) and a clove of garlic. When the oil is golden but before the garlic changes colour, remove the garlic and the chilli and discard. Now add the anchovy fillets and mash them into the oil with a wooden spoon to form a smooth paste.

Strain the pasta and broccoli and transfer to a large dish. Add the anchovy mixture, stir well and serve at once.

Spaghetti con le cozze alla Tarantina
(Spaghetti with mussels, Tarantina style) **

Taranto, or Taras as it was known, was one of the most opulent and famous of all the cities of Magna Graecia, founded by the shamed sons of Sparta in search of a new beginning. The remains lie beneath the modern city but the National Museum is full of sophisticated jewellery and delightful statuary that confirm a history that her city streets deny.

The old town is a maze of tiny roads and alleys criss-crossing a spit of land bordered on one side by the sea and on the other by a lagoon. The Mar Piccolo teems with tiny craft tending the famous mussel and oyster beds and the quaysides that face the lagoon are noisy and dusty and filled with fish stalls and fishermen. Tables tucked in behind the fish stalls serve piles of shellfish, *la zuppa di pesce* and other local specialities, plus a never-ending variety of fish plucked straight from the sea and plunged into the pan.

Fresh mussels are wonderfully cheap and delicious when in season, so make the most of them! They will keep for at least 36 hours in a bucket of cold water in a cool place. Be sure to discard any that are not tightly shut before they are cooked and any that are not open once they have been cooked. Scrub them well and rinse them well before cooking and you will have no problems.

400 g (1 lb) spaghetti
1 kg (2 lb) fresh plump mussels
half a wine glass and 2 tbs extra
virgin olive oil (from Puglia if
possible)
1 heaped tbs onion, finely chopped

1 clove of garlic, finely chopped
1 wine glass of dry white wine
salt and pepper
1 heaped tbs parsley, finely
chopped

Scrub the mussels, pull away the beard and rinse in cold water until perfectly clean. If there are any barnacles attached scrape them off with a sharp knife, as they will free themselves in the heat of the cooking pot and ruin the dish.

Pour the half wine glass of oil into a large heavy-based pan. I use a wok, but in Taranto they use a large earthenware pot. Add the onion and garlic and cook over a low heat until transparent. Increase the heat, add the wine and a grinding of pepper and heat through. Add the mussels, cover with a lid and cook over a very high heat. Shake the pan from time to time until they have all opened. Any that remain closed should be discarded.

Lift the mussels out of the pan with a slotted spoon and discard half the shells only (the clink of the mussel shells is part of the charm of the dish) and set on one side. Strain the pan juices to remove any sand or grit and reduce by half.

Bring a large pan of salted water to the boil. Pour in the pasta and cook *al dente*. Strain the pasta and return to the pan, add the 2 tablespoons of olive oil and 2 tablespoons of pasta water and mix well. Add the pan juices, the mussels and half the chopped parsley and stir again.

Pour the pasta on to a wide serving dish, sprinkle with the remaining parsley and serve at once.

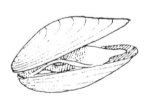

PASTA PRESTO

Quick and Simple

Here is a collection of simple pasta dishes that can be prepared in next to no time with storecupboard ingredients or from a few ounces of left-over poultry, meat or fish. There are other recipes that fit into these categories which appear in other chapters of the book and are marked with a single star and with the storecupboard sign where appropriate.

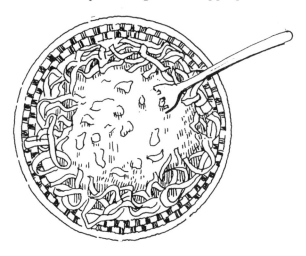

Tagliatelle con pollo, panna e dragoncello
(Tagliatelle with chicken, cream and tarragon) ✳

250 g (10 oz) tagliatelle	*4 tbs freshly grated parmesan*
125 ml (¼ pint) single cream	*1 tbs fresh chopped tarragon*
125 ml (¼ pint) yogurt	*100 g (4 oz) flaked cold chicken*
50 g (2 oz) butter	*salt and pepper to taste*

Bring a large pan of salted water to the boil. Pour in the pasta and cook *al dente*.

Gently heat the cream and yogurt, the butter and the parmesan together. Add the chopped tarragon to the cream and allow it to stand for a while.

As soon as the pasta is ready strain it and transfer it to a large serving dish, add the small pieces of chicken, the cream sauce, a grinding of black pepper and 2 tablespoons of pasta water. Stir well and serve at once.

Penne con pollo al curry
(Quills with curried chicken) *

400 g (1 lb) pasta quills
olive oil
1 small piece ginger root 1 cm
(½ in) square, 1 small piece chilli
1 cm (½ in) square and ½ clove of
garlic, combined and finely
chopped
2 crushed coriander seeds
a pinch each of turmeric, cumin
and cardamon
100 g (4 oz) cold cooked chicken,
chopped into small pieces
250 ml (½ pint) yogurt
half a fresh mango or two fresh
apricots, cut into small pieces
salt
1 or 2 poppadoms

Stir-fry the ginger, chilli and garlic in a little oil on a high heat for 1 minute, then add the spices, turn once and reduce the heat. Add the chicken and cook for a further minute. Reduce the heat to very low, add the yogurt to the pan and heat through for 5 minutes to allow the flavours to blend. Add the chopped mango or apricots.

Meanwhile bring a large pan of salted water to the boil. Pour in the pasta and cook *al dente*.

Strain the pasta and transfer to a large serving dish, add the yogurt mixture and stir well. Lightly crush the poppadoms and sprinkle the pieces over the pasta. Serve at once.

Spaghetti coi piselli e la carne arrosto
(Spaghetti with peas, dill and roast meat) *

This dish is based on a recipe by the great Artusi who recommended it as a good and tasty family meal. He used dried meat and fresh peas but I have adapted it to use up left-over scraps of roast meat and frozen peas.

400 g (1 lb) spaghetti
1 small onion
1 clove of garlic
1 stick of celery
a few sprigs of parsley
2 tbs olive oil
400 g (1 lb) frozen peas
a few sprigs of dill, chopped
salt and pepper
100 g (4 oz) left-over roast meat
butter
2 tbs parmesan cheese, freshly
grated

Chop the onion, garlic, celery and parsley together very finely. Heat the olive oil in a saucepan, add the chopped vegetables and simmer over a low heat until transparent. Add the peas and dill, and salt and pepper to taste, and continue to cook over a low heat until tender. Cut the meat into matchstick strips and add to the peas. Mix well and heat through thoroughly.

Bring a large pan of salted water to the boil. Pour in the pasta and cook *al dente*.

Strain the pasta and transfer to a large serving dish, add a knob of butter, the pea sauce and the parmesan cheese, stir well and serve at once.

Tortiglioni con prosciutto cotto, fagiolini e mascarpone
(Pasta tubes with cooked ham, French beans and mascarpone cheese) *

The Italians have many appetizing and unusual ways of using cooked ham. These come into their own at festive times of the year when the essential ham sometimes outstays its welcome! There are some delicious pasta sauces to be made by simply adding slivers of cooked ham, peas, French beans, or even asparagus to cream or cream cheese.

400 g (1 lb) tortiglioni	1 bay leaf
200 g (8 oz) mascarpone cheese or	100 g (4 oz) French beans
100 g (4 oz) soft cream cheese	50 g (2 oz) butter
mixed with 100 g (4 oz) single	100 g (4 oz) cooked ham, chopped
cream	2 tbs parmesan cheese
4 cloves	salt and pepper

Gently warm the mascarpone with the cloves and the bay leaf and leave it to stand for an hour. Cut the French beans in half and cook them in a little salted water until tender.

Bring a large pan of salted water to the boil. Pour in the pasta and cook *al dente*.

Remove the cloves and the bay leaf from the mascarpone, then add the butter, ham and beans and heat through gently. Strain the pasta and transfer to a large serving dish. Add the mascarpone mixture, 2 tablespoons of pasta water, the parmesan and a grinding of black pepper. Stir well and serve at once.

Tagliatelle al prosciutto cotto, porri e bacche di ginepro
(Tagliatelle with ham, leeks, cream and juniper berries) *

250 g (10 oz) tagliatelle	250 ml (½ pint) single cream
100 g (4 oz) cooked ham	salt and pepper
100 g (4 oz) leek (white part only)	2 tbs parmesan cheese, freshly
50 g (2 oz) butter	grated
5 crushed juniper berries	

Cut the ham and the leeks into matchstick strips. Melt the butter in a heavy-based pan and sweat the leek strips until tender. Add the ham, the juniper berries, the cream and a grinding of black pepper and allow them to heat through gently.

Bring a large pan of salted water to the boil. Pour in the pasta and cook *al dente*.

Strain the pasta and transfer to a large serving dish. Add the sauce, 2 tablespoons of pasta water and the parmesan. Stir well and serve at once.

Tagliatelle con nocciole, germogli e maiale
(Tagliatelle with hazelnuts, beansprouts and pork) *

250 g (10 oz) tagliatelle	3 tbs olive oil
50 g (2 oz) hazelnuts	salt and pepper
150 g (6 oz) cold roast pork	50 g (2 oz) parmesan cheese
400 g (1 lb) beansprouts	

Toast the hazelnuts under a hot grill until brown all over. When they have cooled a little place them in a small bag and crush them with a rolling pin. Cut the cold meat into strips 2 cm by 1 cm (¾ in by ½ in). Stir-fry the beansprouts in hot oil for 1 minute, then add the pork strips and stir-fry until heated through. Add salt and plenty of black pepper.

Bring a large pan of salted water to the boil. Pour in the pasta and cook *al dente*.

Strain the pasta and transfer to a large serving dish. Add the beansprouts and pork, parmesan cheese and toasted hazelnuts. Stir well and serve at once.

Torta di pasta fritta
(Fried pasta pie) * ●

Here are two ideas for using up left-over pasta. This recipe however starts from scratch with freshly-cooked pasta, for those of you who, like us, rarely have any left! Left-over pasta can also be reheated in the microwave if covered tightly.

200 g (8 oz) spaghetti	2 anchovy fillets (omit the anchovy
half a wine glass of olive oil	if using left-over pasta that has
1 clove of garlic	already been mixed with a sauce)

Bring a large pan of salted water to the boil. Pour in the pasta and cook *al dente*.

In a large, heavy-based frying pan, gently cook the garlic in the olive oil until golden. Remove the garlic and discard. Add the anchovy fillets and break them up with a fork.

Strain the pasta thoroughly. Add the oil and anchovy, mix well and tip into the frying pan. Flatten it to form a solid mass, increase the heat and fry until it forms a brown crust. Tip the 'pie' out onto an oiled plate, slide it back into the pan and fry until it forms a crust on the other side.

Alternatively the pan can be oiled and lined with breadcrumbs, giving the 'pie' a crustier finish. Do not forget to re-oil and re-line the frying pan with breadcrumbs before returning the pie to it to cook the other side. Serve at once cut into slices on a warm plate.

Spaghetti alle vongole
(Quick spaghetti with clams) * ●

This is a very colourful and attractive dish: the marble white of the clams, the rich red of the tomatoes and the field-fresh green of the parsley echo the colours of the Italian flag. It makes an excellent storecupboard dish as the only fresh ingredient is the parsley. If I do not have any in the garden I make sure I have some in a jar on the kitchen windowsill and some in the freezer. It is a popular supper dish in our family, made without the chilli.

400 g (1 lb) thin spaghetti	1 small piece of chilli (optional)
2 tbs olive oil	1 tin baby clams
400 g (1 lb) tinned plum tomatoes	1 handful of parsley, chopped
drained, deseeded and chopped	salt and pepper to taste
1 clove of garlic	

Place the olive oil, tomato pieces, garlic and chilli if required in a pan and simmer over a low heat until the sauce becomes thick and creamy (20 to 30 minutes). Add the strained clam juice to the pan and simmer for a further 10 minutes or so to reduce the sauce. Then add the clams and allow them to warm through.

While the sauce reduces, bring a large pan of salted water to the boil. Pour in the pasta and cook al dente.

Strain the pasta and transfer to a large serving dish. Add the clam sauce and the chopped parsley, stir well and serve at once. Do not add parmesan.

Conchighlie al tonno, cipolla e corianderlo
(Pasta shells with tuna, onion and coriander) * ●

Most storecupboards run to a couple of onions and a tin of tuna on the leanest of days, which makes this the ideal meal for an unexpected visitor. It is an inexpensive dish to produce and its mild creamy taste makes it popular as a supper dish for all the family.

> 400 g (1 lb) pasta shells
> 2 medium-sized onions
> 1 tbs olive oil
> 1 tbs butter
> 1 tsp crushed coriander seeds

> 1 200 g (8 oz) tin tuna fish
> 1 tbs tomato purée
> 3 tbs milk
> salt and pepper to taste

Peel the onions and slice them finely. Melt the olive oil and butter in a large frying pan, add the onion and a tablespoon of warm water and cook over a low heat until very tender, taking care not to allow them to discolour. Crush the coriander seeds with a pestle and mortar (or by putting them in a small plastic bag or small bowl and crushing them with the end of a rolling pin). Add the coriander to the pan and stir well.

Flake the tuna and add it to the sauce together with the tomato purée, milk and salt and black pepper to taste. Stir again, cover and allow to cook for at least 10 minutes over a very low heat to allow the flavours to blend.

Bring a large pan of salted water to the boil. Pour in the pasta and cook *al dente*. Strain the pasta and transfer to a large serving dish. Add the tuna sauce, stir well and serve at once. (Parmesan cheese is not generally served with fish sauces.)

Rigatoni con funghi secchi, timo e la besciamella
(Rigatoni with dried mushrooms, thyme and béchamel sauce) ** ●

The tiny and rather costly packets of dried porcini mushrooms are useful in recreating the exquisite pasta sauces traditional in the *boschi* (wood-lands) around Rome and other major Italian cities. A fresh porcino mushroom has an exquisite and distinctive flavour and texture and is best cooked simply in a little olive oil, parsley and garlic and then added to the pasta. The dried version however needs to be served in a sauce to obtain the best results. They are excellent stewed with garlic, butter and herbs and added to meat, cream and béchamel sauces.

This is an excellent way of capturing the flavour of wild porcini mush-rooms with a packet of dried ones. A starter or main meal to delight vegetarians and meat-eaters alike!

> 400 g (1 lb) rigatoni
> 40 g (2 oz) dried porcini
> mushrooms
> 1 tbs butter
> 1 tbs olive oil
> a few sprigs of fresh thyme

> 1 clove of garlic, chopped
> a little stock
> parmesan cheese
> 1 quantity of béchamel sauce
> (see page 23)

Soak and dry the mushrooms (see page 114). Melt the butter with the oil in a large pan over a gentle heat. Add the mushrooms, the thyme leaves (removed from their stalks) and the garlic. Cook over a low heat until tender (20 minutes). Add a little warm stock from time to time if the mushrooms dry out.

Prepare the béchamel sauce.

Bring a large pan of salted water to the boil. Pour in the pasta and cook *al dente*.

Strain the pasta and return to the pan. Add the mushrooms and the béchamel sauce, stir well and serve at once with plenty of freshly grated parmesan.

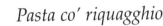

Pasta co' riquagghio

(Maccheroni with eggs, pecorino cheese and parsley) *

Eggs are one of the oldest foods known to man and the most convenient known to woman! Sadly eggs have in recent years had a bad press. I love eggs cooked any way except hard boiled, which according to many sources is the only safe way to eat them. If you are of that opinion then the following recipe will certainly not appeal.

This Sicilian speciality can be made in next to no time which makes it an easy supper dish for the unexpected guest.

400 g (1 lb) maccheroni	*6 tbs good olive oil*
a handful of parsley	*3 tbs grated pecorino cheese*
4 eggs	*(parmesan will do)*
salt and pepper	

Bring a large pan of salted water to the boil. Pour in the pasta and cook *al dente*.

Chop the parsley. Beat the eggs and add salt and a grinding of pepper to taste. Just before the pasta is ready heat the olive oil in a wide-based pan, large enough to hold the pasta. Strain the pasta, then pour it into the hot olive oil and mix rapidly for a minute or two. Add a stream of beaten egg and the cheese and mix well.

Remove from the heat and add the chopped parsley. Stir well and serve at once.

Tagliatelle con noci e aglio
(Tagliatelle with walnuts and garlic) *

This is my adaptation of a regional dish from Piedmont called agliata. It is usually served in the autumn when the new wine is tapped and tasted.

400 g (1 lb) narrow tagliatelle
50 g (2 oz) shelled walnuts
1 clove of garlic
50 g (2 oz) butter

parmesan cheese
250 ml (½ pint) single cream
salt and pepper

Chop the walnuts and garlic finely. This can be done with a pestle and mortar or in an electric chopper or food processor, but take care not to reduce the walnuts too much or they will lose their nutty texture. Melt the butter, parmesan and cream over a low heat, shaking the pan from time to time until the mixture has heated through and thickened a little.

Bring a large pan of salted water to the boil. Pour in the pasta and cook al dente.

When the pasta is ready strain it and transfer it to a large serving dish. Add the cream sauce, 2 tablespoons of pasta water and half the walnut mixture, stir well and serve at once sprinkled with the remaining nuts.

Pasta estiva
(Summer pasta) *

This is an unusual sauce, in which the tomatoes and herbs are 'cooked' in a marinade of olive oil and served with hot, freshly-cooked pasta as a cooling summer starter. A similar dish can be made using up left-over green salad that has been dressed in olive oil and lemon juice. Stir it into the freshly cooked pasta with matchstick-sized strips of lemon zest.

400 g (1 lb) spaghetti
300 g (12 oz) ripe tomatoes
a mixed bunch of mint, parsley and
basil

1 clove of garlic, crushed
salt and pepper to taste
slivers of parmesan cheese

Score crosses into the skins of the tomatoes and drop them into boiling water for a few minutes. Remove the skins and the seeds. Chop up the tomatoes and the herbs, and place them in a shallow dish with the garlic. Cover the mixture with olive oil, sprinkle with salt to taste and leave it to stand in a cool place for 48 hours so that it 'cooks' in the oil. It can be marinaded for just the time it takes to cook the pasta, although the flavour will not be quite as good.

Bring a large pan of salted water to the boil. Pour in the pasta and cook *al dente*.

Strain the pasta thoroughly and transfer it to a large serving dish. Add the tomatoes and herbs and a grinding of black pepper. Stir well and serve at once, garnished with a few sprigs of the fresh herbs and a scattering of parmesan slivers.

Pasta con basilico, aglio e olio d'oliva
('Cheat's pesto': pasta with basil, garlic and olive oil) *

If you love the flavour of fresh basil this is a very simple way of serving it to great effect without going to the trouble of making pesto. You can even throw in a few whole toasted pine nuts at the end if you like them.

400 g (1 lb) thin spaghetti	*1 wine glass of olive oil*
36 basil leaves, finely chopped	*2 tbs parmesan cheese*
1 fat clove of garlic, finely chopped	*salt and pepper*

Bring a large pan of salted water to the boil. Pour in the pasta and cook *al dente*.

While the pasta is cooking, gently heat the olive oil in a pan and add the garlic and basil. When warmed through, leave to stand until required.

Strain the pasta and return it to the pan. Add the olive oil, garlic and basil, the parmesan cheese and salt and pepper to taste. Stir well over the heat for 2 minutes and serve at once.

Tagliatelle alla salvia, rosmarino e timo
(Tagliatelle with herb sauce) *

In Italy, town or country, a wide selection of fresh herbs are sold on every greengrocer's stall, fresh in summer and dried in winter. Italians make common use of basil, parsley, oregano, rosemary and sage. Basil, oregano and parsley appear frequently in all sorts of pasta sauces while rosemary and sage are generally used in meat dishes.

This dish makes a delightful summer starter when the herbs are in flower, which incidentally is when they are supposed to have most flavour.

250 g (10 oz) trenette or other
narrow tagliatelle
3 sage leaves
1 sprig of rosemary
1 sprig of thyme
2 tbs chopped parsley

1 clove of garlic
50 g (2 oz) butter
200 g (8 oz) single cream
parmesan
salt and pepper
more parsley

Bring a large pan of salted water to the boil. Pour in the pasta and cook *al dente*.

Chop the herbs and the garlic together finely. Melt the butter in a small pan. Add the garlic and herbs and cook over a very low heat to allow the flavours to diffuse without discolouring the garlic. Add the cream to the pan and allow it to heat through.

As soon as the pasta is ready, strain it and transfer it to a large serving dish. Add the cream sauce, parmesan cheese, more chopped parsley and black pepper. Stir well and serve at once decorated with sprigs of flowering herbs.

Spaghetti da quaresima
(Lenten spaghetti with walnuts and mixed spice) * ●

This very unusual pasta dish is well worth trying. It appeared in Artusi's book written at the turn of the century and combines sweet and sour tastes with spaghetti. Back in the seventeenth century this was not unusual but a hundred years ago the author was afraid it might sound ridiculous.

I liked it, but in its original form I would rather eat it as a pudding than a starter. I have therefore drastically reduced the amount of sugar, which turns the dish into an excellent first course. The original recipe used 30 g (1¼ oz) icing sugar and 1 heaped teaspoon of mixed spice, in case you care to try it.

400 g (1 lb) thin spaghetti
60 g (2½ oz) shelled walnuts
60 g (2½ oz) toasted breadcrumbs

1 level tsp icing sugar
1 level tsp mixed spice
4 tbs good olive oil
black pepper

Crush the walnuts, with either a pestle and mortar or blender. Add the toasted breadcrumbs, the icing sugar and the mixed spice. Meanwhile bring a large pan of salted water to the boil. Pour in the pasta and cook *al dente*. Heat the olive oil until it smokes.

Strain the pasta and transfer to a large serving dish. Add the boiling hot olive oil and plenty of black pepper and stir well. Add the dry ingredients, mix well and serve at once.

PASTA E PESCE

Seafood Sauces

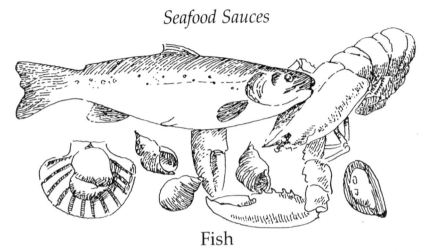

Fish

Fish is good for us – our mothers told us so! Yet it is not really popular. Is that because we know it's good for us, or because it's full of fiddly bones, or because we lack imagination when it comes to cooking it?

Most fresh fish is eaten grilled, poached or fried. Kedgeree and fish pies made with pastry and mashed potato are also traditional and delicious, but the fish soups, stews and sauces so popular in the Mediterranean are seldom encountered here.

I lived in Cornwall for years and watched huge French container lorries queuing nightly at the harbour to whisk away lobsters, crayfish and scallops to eagerly awaiting customers in France and Spain, who are willing to pay top prices for such manna.

With the advent of the super-supermarket selling the most popular kinds of fresh fish, fishmongers are becoming a rarity. This is a great shame, as a visit to a good fish shop brings instant inspiration for the weekend's eating. A good fishmonger knows a great deal about the fish he sells and how to cook it, and is always willing to advise when called upon, waiting customers permitting. If you have enjoyed fabulous seafood abroad or drool over the fish sections of books on foreign food, look beyond your local supermarket. There is probably a good fish shop somewhere in your area.

Freshwater fish, shellfish, white fish and smoked fish can all be used in pasta sauces, given a little thought and the right additions. I have included many recipes using my favourite fish, but don't be afraid to experiment with other kinds.

Spaghetti con mandorle tostate, trota e timo
(Spaghetti with toasted almonds, trout and thyme) **

This dish is a combination of a classic Venetian recipe for trout and the British trout and almonds. It is a delicious fish dish ideal for a supper party or special family meal. The trout is wrapped in a buttered paper parcel together with herbs, vegetables and lemon juice and can be either grilled or microwaved. This traditional Italian way of cooking fish is known as *al cartoccio*. I thoroughly recommend cooking any kind of fish this way.

400 g (1 lb) spaghetti	*50 g (2 oz) butter*
300 g (12 oz) trout (raw weight)	*salt and pepper*
2 sticks of celery	*25 g (1 oz) almonds, toasted and*
1 large carrot	*crushed*
a few sprigs of thyme	*tinfoil or greaseproof paper*
lemon	

Ask the fishmonger to gut the trout, leaving the head on. Wash the fish and dry it inside and out, then place a sprig of thyme and a slice of lemon inside. Clean the celery and carrot and cut into matchstick pieces.

Take a piece of tinfoil (if using the grill) or greaseproof paper (if using a microwave oven) large enough to enclose the fish. Butter the paper generously, lay the vegetable strips in the middle and place the fish on top. Add salt and pepper to taste. Wrap up the trout, taking care to seal the edges to stop the juices escaping.

Put the tinfoil parcel under a medium to hot grill for 8 minutes, turning it over halfway through the cooking time. If using the microwave, place the parcel on a plate and microwave on high for 3 to 4 minutes.

Unwrap the fish and check it is cooked through by opening the flesh along the spine with a knife. If the flesh looks at all pink put it back to cook for a minute or two longer, but do take care not to overcook it.

When the fish is cooked, put the vegetable strips on one side. Remove the skin, take the flesh off the bone and break it up with a fork. Mix the fish with the vegetable strips and set on one side until the pasta is ready.

Bring a large pan of salted water to the boil. Pour in the pasta and cook *al dente*.

Strain the pasta and transfer to a large serving dish. Add the remaining butter, three quarters of the toasted almonds, the flaked fish, the vegetable strips and half a teaspoon of fresh thyme leaves and stir well. Garnish with the remaining almonds and sprigs of flowering thyme when in season. Serve at once.

Spaghetti alle vongole in bianco
(Spaghetti with fresh clams) **

This spaghetti dish from Campania is another of my favourites. Fresh clams are not easy to come by, although their tiny white, smooth, fan-shaped shells lie in thousands on many of our beaches. It is worth keeping an eye open for them in some of the bigger, more adventurous fish shops and market stalls. In the fish markets of the Mediterranean they are to be bought in various sizes and are sold from vast shallow trays of sea water. They fascinate my children who love to watch them opening and closing and squirting jets of water with their miniature trunks.

The very smallest clams are the sweetest and most tender, and it is these that the Italians use for this recipe. Don't be put off buying them just because they are small – you clean them by rinsing them in plenty of running water, cook them and serve them in the shells. Your guests will do the rest!

If you cannot find fresh baby clams, the canned variety is readily available, sometimes complete with shells. These are perfect, because part of the charm of this dish is the chink of the shells on the plate. Many years ago, while dining *al fresco* at a quayside restaurant in Positano after a long absence from Italy, I was enthusing about the joys of eating a plate of *spaghetti alle vongole* complete with shells. My normally cool husband was somewhat taken aback when *all'improvviso* I asked the waiter if I could have the empty shells that were left on our plates. Nothing is too much trouble in a restaurant in Italy; by the time we had finished our meal the shells were returned to me, clean, odourless and discreetly wrapped, ready to be added to my hitherto shell-less clam spaghetti.

There are two ways of serving spaghetti with clams. One is *in bianco* (literally 'in white') with olive oil and garlic; this is the best way of serving fresh clams. The other way is *al pomodoro* (in tomato sauce), excellent for the canned variety (see page 61).

400 g (1 lb) spaghetti	1 clove of garlic
1 kg (2½ lb) fresh clams in their shells	a piece of chilli (optional)
3 tbs good olive oil	a handful of parsley

Wash the clams in plenty of running salted water and strain well. Place them in a large, thick-bottomed pan (I use a wok). With the lid on, shake the pan over high heat until all the clams have opened.

Now remove the clams with a slotted spoon and rinse them in warm salted water to remove any remaining sand. Drain them well. Reduce the pan juices to half and put them through a muslin-lined sieve.

Place the olive oil in a large pan, together with the clove of garlic and the chilli, if desired. Heat through until the garlic turns gold, then remove the chilli and the garlic and add the clams, pan juices and parsley.

Bring a large pan of salted water to the boil. Pour in the pasta and cook *al dente*.

Strain the pasta and transfer to a large serving dish. Add the clams and the boiling hot juices. Stir well, sprinkle with a tablespoon of chopped parsley and serve at once. Parmesan is not required.

Spaghetti con telline e funghi secchi
(Spaghetti with cockles and dried mushrooms) **

Cockles are a northern European speciality and figure as part of the traditional British seaside scene, sold ready-cooked from promenade stalls along with mussels, prawns and whelks. Cockles are not as popular in Italy as clams and mussels, but they are not uncommon. If you are using fresh cockles this dish requires quite some preparation, but with ready-cooked shelled cockles it is quick and easy to make.

400 g (1 lb) spaghetti	1 carrot
1500 g (3¾ lb) whole cockles or	1 stick of celery
250 g (10 oz) shelled	1 small onion
a few pieces of dried mushroom,	2 tbs olive oil
soaked (see page 114)	1 tbs butter
garlic	salt
parsley	

Wash the cockles well and scrub them if necessary. To remove the sand, place an upturned dish in the bottom of a bucket of cold salt water. Add the cockles and leave to soak for 2 hours. Remove the cockles carefully, taking care not to disturb the sand that has settled at the bottom. Drain well.

Pour them into a large heavy-based pan. Cover with water, bring to the boil and simmer until all the shells have opened. Take the cockles from the pan with a slotted spoon, discarding any that remain closed. Remove them from their shells and set on one side. Strain the water to ensure there is no sand left at the bottom, as this will be used for cooking the spaghetti.

Chop together the garlic, parsley, carrot, celery and onion very finely, reserving a little parsley for the garnish. Heat the olive oil and butter in a frying pan and add the *battuto*. Simmer over a low heat until transparent. Squeeze the excess water from the mushrooms and pat them dry.

Now add the cockles and mushrooms, a little salt and pepper to taste, and cook over a low heat for half an hour. Add a little of the cockle water to the sauce as it is cooking to keep it moist.

Bring the cockle water plus enough tap water to fill your pasta pan to the boil (add salt to taste). Pour in the pasta and cook *al dente*.

Strain the pasta and transfer to a large serving dish. Add the cockles, stir well, sprinkle with chopped parsley and serve at once.

Spaghetti con merluzzo, pomodoro e marsala
(Spaghetti with cod, tomato and Marsala wine) **

Any white fish can be used for this dish and sherry can be substituted for the Marsala wine. This is one of Artusi's recipes.

400 g (1 lb) thin spaghetti	*4 tbs Marsala wine*
1 small onion	*3 tbs fresh tomato sauce (see*
2 tbs olive oil	*page 23) or 1 tsp tomato conserve*
300 g (¾ lb) cod or whiting	*(see page 24)*
a grating of nutmeg	*a handful of chopped parsley*

Chop the onion finely. Heat the oil and cook the onion until transparent. Add the cod, salt to taste, and a grating of nutmeg. Cook gently for 2 minutes.

Now add the Marsala and allow it to warm through. Add the tomato sauce and cook over a very low heat with the lid on for 10 minutes. Then remove the fish from the pan, discard the skin and bones, fork the flesh lightly to break it up and put it back in the sauce to reheat.

Bring a large pan of salted water to the boil. Pour in the pasta and cook *al dente*.

Strain the pasta and transfer to a large serving dish. Add the fish sauce and a handful of chopped parsley, stir well and serve at once.

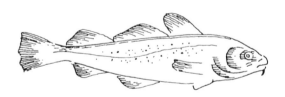

Anguilla in umido con polenta
(Eel stewed in herbs and wine vinegar with polenta) ✳✳

Until the eighteenth century eel stew was popular everywhere but today only jellied and smoked eels are really appreciated. Eels were a common catch in the local lake when we were children, but only our Italian cow man Andrew took them home to stew – everyone else threw them back.

The best eel in the whole of Italy comes from Comacchio in Romagna, where it is a speciality served in all manner of ways: grilled, roasted, casseroled, in fish soup or with polenta. The eels come in a variety of sizes, from the gigantic fully grown beast to the minute elver, which is plunged live into boiling hot oil and eaten like whitebait.

This dish is based on a recipe in Anna Gosetti della Salda's book *Le Recette Regionali Italiane*. In the section on Emilia Romagna she lists eight different ways of cooking eel. If eel is unavailable any other solid white fish will do. Monkfish cheeks are perfect.

1 kg (2 lb) eel or monkfish cheeks	*1 bay leaf*
1 tbs butter	*1 sage leaf*
2 tbs olive oil	*a handful of parsley, finely chopped*
1 small onion, finely chopped	*a clove of garlic, finely chopped*
a little wine vinegar	*1 stick of celery, finely chopped*
a pinch of mace	*salt and pepper*
1 tsp tomato purée	

Ask the fishmonger to gut the eel and remove the head. Wash and skin the eel and cut it into 6–7 cm (2 in) cubes. Heat the butter and olive oil over a low heat, add the finely chopped onion and fry until transparent. Sprinkle the onion with the wine vinegar and add a pinch of mace, a grinding of black pepper and a teaspoon of tomato purée dissolved in a wine glass of warm water. Stir well and warm through.

Add the pieces of eel, the bay and sage leaves and the finely chopped parsley, celery and garlic. Add salt to taste. Cover the pan and cook very slowly for 30 minutes. Shake the pan to prevent sticking; don't stir the fish or the flesh will fall to pieces.

Serve hot with freshly made polenta (see page 22).

Spaghetti ai frutti di mare
(Spaghetti with seafood sauce) **

This sauce is based on the traditional *zuppa di pesce* (fish soup) from Taranto, served not with pasta but with slices of French bread toasted in the oven. There are many regional variations on this recipe but I have chosen this one because Taranto's reputation for the freshness, flavour and variety of its catch is second to none.

If you do not have access to a good fish shop you can buy packs of mixed ready-cooked shellfish and add it to the cod. Although not as tasty as fresh shellfish it still makes an excellent spaghetti sauce.

400 g (1 lb) spaghetti	*300 g (12 oz) cod, boned and cut*
800 g (2 lb) mixed seafood in its	*into pieces (or fresh eel, if*
shells (mussels, cockles,	*available)*
clams, etc.)	*salt and pepper*
olive oil	*a handful of parsley, finely chopped*
2 cloves of garlic, finely chopped	*3 tinned plum tomatoes, drained,*
200 g (8 oz) whole prawns (raw if	*deseeded and chopped*
available)	

Wash the shellfish and place them in a large, heavy-based pan. Cover and cook over a high heat for a few minutes until the shells have opened. Discard any that do not open.

Heat a wine glass of olive oil, add the finely-chopped garlic and cook over a low heat for a minute or two. Add the mixed shellfish and stir well; if using raw prawns they should be added now rather than at the end. Then add the cod, salt and pepper, three quarters of the parsley and the tomatoes and cook over a low heat until the cod is cooked through.

If you are using cooked prawns, heat a little olive oil with a crushed clove of garlic and stir-fry the prawns on a high heat for 2 minutes. Add them to the other fish.

Bring a large pan of salted water to the boil. Pour in the pasta and cook *al dente*.

Strain the pasta and transfer to a large serving dish. Add the fish sauce and a tablespoon of chopped parsley, stir well and serve at once. (Parmesan is not generally served with fish sauces.)

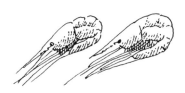

Spaghetti con cape sante, zenzero e aglio di serpe
(Spaghetti with scallops, ginger and chives) *

400 g (1 lb) very thin spaghetti	1 tbs olive oil
400 g (1 lb) scallops	salt and pepper
lemon juice	half a glass of white wine
2 cm (1 in) chunk of fresh root	a bunch of chives or 2 spring onion
ginger	tops
50 g (2 oz) butter	

Clean the scallops and pull the corals carefully away from the white fish. Rinse the corals in cold water, pat dry and set on one side. Wash and dry the whites of the scallops, cut them in half horizontally, and then into quarters. Sprinkle them with a few drops of lemon juice. Peel the ginger and chop it very finely.

Melt the butter with the oil in a frying pan and lightly fry the ginger for 1 minute. Add the scallops to the pan, add salt and pepper to taste and fry until golden on both sides. Cut the corals into three or four pieces, depending on their size. Increase the heat under the scallops and add the wine. When the wine starts to bubble, add the corals and cook for another minute.

Bring a large pan of salted water to the boil. Pour in the pasta and cook *al dente*.

Strain the pasta and transfer to a large serving dish. Add the scallops and pan juices, 2 tablespoons of pasta water and the chopped chives or spring onion tops, stir well and serve at once.

Spaghetti con sarde e semi di finocchio
(Spaghetti with fennel seeds and sardines) ** ●

This recipe is based on the Sicilian way of cooking oily fish with fennel seeds. Fresh anchovy or tuna or even canned tuna and sardines can be used as alternatives to fresh sardines. This dish makes a popular family meal.

400 g (1 lb) spaghetti	2 tins of sardines in brine
2 cloves of garlic	1/2 tbs fennel seeds
1 small onion	salt and pepper
4 tbs olive oil	white wine
400 g (1 lb) fresh sardines or	

Chop the garlic and onion very finely. Heat the olive oil over a low heat, add the onion and garlic and cook until transparent. Take care not to allow them to colour.

Meanwhile clean the sardines, remove the heads and spines, and add them to the pan together with the fennel seeds. Add salt and pepper to taste and enough white wine to cover them. Simmer for 5 minutes, stirring very carefully.

If using canned sardines, add the fennel seeds and the wine to the onion and allow the wine to evaporate a little before adding the sardines, which should first be lightly mashed with a fork.

Bring a large pan of salted water to the boil. Pour in the pasta and cook *al dente*.

Strain the pasta and transfer to a large serving dish, add the sardines, stir well and serve at once.

Tagliatelle con salmone
(Tagliatelle with salmon) *

This is a very simple dish that can be prepared in the time it takes to cook the pasta. It makes a few ounces of salmon go a long way, as a delicate starter for a summer party or a special supper dish for all the family. It is also an excellent way of using up elegant leftovers! Smoked salmon pieces can be used instead of fresh salmon, but do not heat them in the cream as smoked salmon loses something if it is cooked. Simply chop it up into little strips and stir it in after the cream sauce has been added.

250 g (10 oz) tagliatelle	salt and pepper
50 g (2 oz) butter	1 tsp chopped fennel
200 ml (½ pint) single cream	more fennel to garnish
150 g (6 oz) fresh salmon, lightly	parmesan cheese (optional)
poached or microwaved	

Bring a large pan of salted water to the boil. Put the butter and cream in a small pan and heat very gently, shaking the pan from time to time until the butter has melted and the cream has warmed through. Flake the salmon with a fork, making sure that all the bones have been removed. Add the salmon to the cream, season with salt and pepper to taste, add the chopped fennel and leave over a very low heat for the flavours to mix.

When the water comes to the boil, pour in the pasta and cook *al dente*.

Strain the pasta and transfer to a large serving dish. Add the salmon and cream, stir well and serve at once, sprinkled with the remaining fennel and with parmesan cheese if desired.

Spaghetti con muggine e coriandolo
(Spaghetti with red mullet and fresh coriander) **

If you are unable to buy red mullet, use your favourite white fish in its stead. Coriander is a pretty, feathery herb found all around the Mediterranean but it is associated with Middle Eastern rather than Mediterranean food. I discovered its warm peppery aroma while in the Algarve, where it is used as commonly as parsley and basil are used in Italy.

400 g (1 lb) thin spaghetti
150 g (6 oz) red mullet, cooked
weight
2 tbs and a half wine glass of olive
oil

lemon
1 clove of garlic, crushed
salt and pepper
a bunch of fresh coriander

Marinade the whole fish in 2 tablespoons of olive oil and 1 of lemon juice with the garlic. Add salt and a grinding of black pepper and a few stalks of coriander. Cover and leave to stand for at least 2 hours, turning once.

Wrap the fish in oiled paper with a slice of lemon and the coriander stalks and bake at 160°C (320°F, gas 2/3) for 15 minutes or microwave for 3 or 4 minutes. Unwrap the fish and gently insert a knife to ensure it has cooked through. If not, return it to the oven for a little longer.

Set aside the cooking juices. Lift the flesh from the bone and add it to the juices. The liver of the red mullet is considered a luxury and may be removed, chopped finely and added to the fish. The fish can be prepared to this stage well in advance and kept in the fridge until required.

Bring a large pan of salted water to the boil. Pour in the pasta and cook *al dente*.

Heat the half wine glass of olive oil in a small pan, add to it the mullet and the cooking juices and heat through. Add half the chopped coriander and stir.

Strain the pasta and transfer to a large serving dish. Add the mullet and 2 tablespoons of pasta water, stir well and serve at once sprinkled with the remaining coriander. Do not add parmesan cheese.

Tagliarini, sogliola, zafferano e panna
(Thin tagliatelle with sole, saffron and cream) **

250 g (10 oz) narrow tagliatelle
50 g (2 oz) butter
300 g (12 oz) fillets of sole
half a glass of white wine
a pinch of saffron soaked in

2 tbs of warm water
salt and pepper
200 ml (8 fl oz) single cream
2 tbs chopped chives

Melt the butter and cook the fillets of sole briskly, face side down, and then skin side down, until the flesh is set, about a minute on either side. Add the white wine, the saffron and half the chopped chives, a little salt and a grinding of black pepper. Cover and simmer for 2 minutes.

Remove the fish from the pan, flake it carefully with a fork and discard the skin and bones. Place on one side. Reduce the pan juices by half over a high heat. Reduce heat to low, add the cream and the fish and warm through.

Bring a large pan of salted water to the boil. Pour in the pasta and cook *al dente*.

Strain the pasta and transfer to a large serving dish, add the sole and cream sauce, 2 tablespoons of pasta water and the chopped chives, stir well and serve at once.

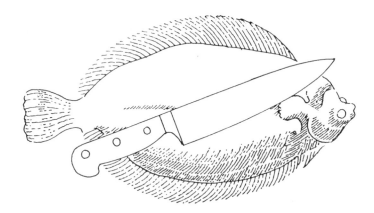

PASTA E VERDURA
Rich vegetable dishes

Farfalle, carciofi, prezzemolo e panna
(Butterfly pasta with artichokes, parsley and cream) **

The globe artichoke is a member of the thistle family and has been cultivated all over the world for centuries. Pliny, the Roman natural historian, found it strange that people should pay good money for thistles – perhaps he had not tasted them!

As a starter they are absolutely delicious boiled whole and accompanied by a small pot of melted butter, or a bubbling *bagna caöda*, to dip the tender leaves in. They become more and more succulent as you near the heart.

Fresh artichokes are best but they are not always easy to find in peak condition. If you have a garden it is worth trying to grow them. Canned artichoke hearts can be bought in most supermarkets and are useful for making pasta sauces. Soak them in milk first to remove the briny taste. The most successful way of preserving artichokes is in olive oil and good ones are not easy to find except in the very best Italian stores. They are exquisite but expensive and will be best appreciated served with a little crusty bread as a starter rather than in a sauce.

This recipe was given to me by a friend of long standing, Antonia Mazzanti, and makes a delicious dish to serve as a starter for a summer supper party.

400 g (1 lb) pasta bows	1 tbs butter
5 fresh or 8 tinned artichokes	salt and pepper
1 lemon	1 tbs flour
a bunch of parsley	250 ml (½ pint) single cream
1 small onion	50 g (2 fl oz) milk
1 clove of garlic	1 tbs parsley, chopped
4 tbs olive oil	freshly grated parmesan cheese

Clean the fresh artichokes, remove the outer leaves and immerse them in water and lemon juice. Slice the tinned ones thinly and pat dry with absorbent paper, soak in milk and pat dry again.

Chop the parsley, onion and garlic together with a sharp knife until very fine. Heat 1 tablespoon of olive oil and the butter together in a thick-based frying pan, add the *battuto* and cook over a low heat until transparent. Slice the fresh artichokes thinly, add them to the pan and cook for 10 minutes (just heat the tinned ones through). Add a grinding of black pepper, salt to taste and a tablespoon of flour. Stir well and cook for a couple of minutes.

Add the cream and milk and stir until the sauce has thickened, then cover the pan and continue cooking for 20 minutes (10 minutes if using canned artichokes) over a very low heat. Check at intervals that the sauce is not sticking.

Bring a large pan of salted water to the boil. Pour in the pasta and cook *al dente*.

Strain the pasta. Heat 3 tablespoons of olive oil in a very large pan. Add the hot oil, the artichoke mixture and a tablespoon of chopped parsley to the pasta. Mix well over a high heat for a few minutes then pour into a large serving dish and serve at once with plenty of fresh parmesan and pepper to taste.

Penne con asparagi, uova e santoreggia
(Pasta quills with asparagus, egg and savory) *

Our word asparagus comes from the Greek *asparagos*. It was the ancient Greeks who first used the wild plant, which grew all along the Mediterranean coast. The Romans took it into their gardens and cultivated it, but it was not grown elsewhere until the 17th century and it was a long time before it really became the popular vegetable it is today. There are two distinct kinds of asparagus, the white one which is matured underground and the green one that matures in the light.

Asparagus has always been considered a luxury but when it is in season a bundle of tender young spears probably costs less than a dull unripe melon imported at that time of year. So make the most of it when it is in season, but, as with all fresh vegetables, do not buy it if it is not in tip-top condition.

You can buy an asparagus steamer, which like most good kitchen equipment is expensive. If you do not have one, simply stand the asparagus stems in water in a straight-sided ovenproof container covered loosely with a plastic bag, and put the container in a saucepan of boiling water. If you have a microwave oven you can put the container, water, asparagus and plastic bag straight in. It will take 8 or 10 minutes to cook. If cooked immersed in water the asparagus tips disintegrate before the stems are tender.

Asparagus is best eaten in the fingers, served hot with plenty of melted butter and either a grinding of black pepper or a sprinkling of freshly grated parmesan cheese. It can also be accompanied by a dressing of olive oil and lemon juice.

This dish can be served at any occasion in the early summer. It makes a little asparagus go a long way and is very popular with children.

400 g (1 lb) pasta quills	*cheese*
200 g (½ lb) asparagus	*black pepper and salt*
3 eggs	*50 g (2 oz) butter*
125 ml (¼ pint) single cream	*1 tsp chopped savory leaves*
3 tbs grated pecorino or parmesan	

Lightly steam the asparagus until tender, then cut it into pieces 2 cm (1 in) long and discard any tough parts. Bring a large pan of salted water to the boil. Pour in the pasta and cook *al dente*.

Lightly beat the eggs in the bottom of a large serving dish. Add the cream, the grated cheese, a grinding of black pepper and the butter and leave the mixture to stand without stirring until the pasta is ready.

Strain the pasta into the dish containing the egg mixture, add the asparagus pieces and a teaspoon of chopped savory, stir quickly, garnish with a few sprigs of fresh savory and serve at once.

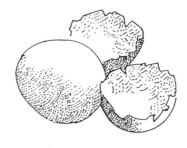

Spaghetti con melanzane, pomodoro, basilico e aglio
(Spaghetti with aubergines, tomato, basil and garlic) **

Aubergines seem to be in the shops most of the year now which means this sauce can be served at any time of year. It makes a tasty supper dish for vegetarians and vegetable lovers.

400 g (1 lb) spaghetti	2 tbs parmesan, freshly grated
3 small aubergines , 400 g (1 lb)	a few stems of basil (use parsley in
in weight, to be prepared 2 hours	winter)
beforehand	1 quantity of tomato sauce
olive oil	(see page 24)
salt and pepper	

Wash the aubergines and slice them thinly. Layer them in a colander, sprinkle with salt, cover with a plate and place a weight on top. Set aside for a couple of hours to allow the bitter liquid to drain away. Pat dry.

Make the tomato sauce.

Deep-fry the slices of aubergine in hot olive oil. Drain on absorbent paper, then sprinkle with salt and pepper.

Bring a large pan of salted water to the boil. Pour in the pasta and cook *al dente*.

Strain the pasta and transfer to a large serving dish. Add the fried aubergines, the tomato sauce and the parmesan cheese. Stir well and serve at once, garnished with freshly chopped herbs.

Timballo di rigatoni, melanzane e mozzarella
(Sicilian aubergine and mozzarella pie) **

Serving a pasta mould is unusual outside Italy, which makes it an ideal party dish. It looks appealing on the table, cloaked in tomato sauce and decorated with fresh herbs. Incidentally, a *timballo* can be made with many different kinds of pasta and flavourings. Try tagliatelle, white sauce, peas and beansprouts, as well as the recipe below.

500 g (1¼ lb) rigatoni or zite	200 g (½ lb) mozzarella
1 quantity tomato sauce	250 ml (½ pint) single cream or
(see page 24)	béchamel sauce (see page 23)
1 tbs fresh or ½ tsp dried oregano	2 tbs freshly grated parmesan
400 g (1 lb) aubergines cut into	toasted breadcrumbs
cubes and salted (see above)	more oregano or chopped parsley to
olive oil	garnish

Prepare the aubergines as described on page 81. Make the tomato sauce, using oregano rather than basil. Heat the oil and fry the aubergines until tender. Dry on absorbent paper. Cut the mozzarella into small cubes. Preheat the oven to 220°C (425°F, gas 7).

Bring a large pan of salted water to the boil. Pour in the pasta and cook *al dente.*

Strain the pasta and return to the pan. Add the aubergines, cream or béchamel sauce, oregano, mozzarella and parmesan cheese. Stir well. Butter a large overproof dish and line with the breadcrumbs. Pour in the dressed pasta and shake the dish gently to settle it. Dot with butter, sprinkle with breadcrumbs and put in the oven for 20 minutes.

Remove the pie from the oven and allow to stand for 5 minutes before turning out onto a serving dish. Pour the tomato sauce over the pie, decorate with fresh oregano leaves or chopped parsley and serve at once, cut into slices.

Farfalle con ricotta, germogli, lattuga e semi di zucca
(Pasta bows with ricotta and beansprouts) *

I do not know if beansprouts have been adopted by the Italians as they have been elsewhere. Anyone enthusiastic about Chinese food will appreciate how well they go with noodles. Although not related as once believed, Italian pasta is not unlike Chinese noodles. This recipe makes a wonderfully refreshing summer starter.

400 g (1 lb) pasta bows	*1 tbs pumpkin seeds*
200 g (8 oz) ricotta cheese	*3 tbs olive oil*
75 g (3 oz) beansprouts	*salt and a grating of nutmeg to*
50 g (2 oz) iceberg lettuce, finely	*taste*
shredded	

Bring a large pan of salted water to the boil, add the pasta and cook *al dente.*

Place all the other ingredients in a large serving bowl, mix well and allow to stand until the pasta is ready. Strain the pasta and add it to the ricotta mixture. Stir well and serve at once.

Bucatini con fave, pomodoro e santoreggia

(Bucatini, broad beans, tomato and savory) ∗

Broad beans are one of my favourite vegetables. They herald the arrival of summer, making a refreshing change from the root vegetables and brassicas that have kept us going through the winter months. Like all fresh vegetables it is essential to buy them in peak condition. If they are bright green, look as though they have just been picked and are not over-large, they should be delicious; if you are in any doubt, leave them in the shop. Broad beans, like peas, go tough when they are old and no amount of cooking can tenderize them. They are, however, one of the few vegetables that freeze fairly successfully – young frozen beans are preferable to old fresh ones. Young, sweet broad beans taste wonderful raw; in Rome they are often eaten with pecorino cheese at the end of a meal, much as we eat cheese with celery.

This summer vegetable dish is quick to make and works well either as a starter or as a main course.

400 g (1 lb) bucatini or spaghetti	½ tbs mild French mustard,
4 spring onions	optional
6 stems of savory	salt and pepper
1 kg (2 lb) fresh broad beans or	400 g (1 lb) tinned plum tomatoes,
250 g (8 oz) frozen	drained, deseeded and cut into
2 tbs olive oil	strips

Chop the spring onions finely. Remove the savory leaves from their stems and chop them roughly. If using fresh beans, boil them until tender but crisp and strain them well. If using the frozen variety simply defrost and dry them.

Heat the oil in a wok or large frying pan. Add the onion and stir-fry on high for 1 minute. Lower the heat and add the broad beans, mustard, salt and pepper and stir-fry again for 1 minute. Add the tomato strips and chopped savory and cook for a further 2 or 3 minutes to allow the flavours to blend.

Bring a large pan of salted water to the boil. Pour in the pasta and cook *al dente*.

Strain the pasta and transfer to a large serving dish. Add the sauce, stir well and serve at once.

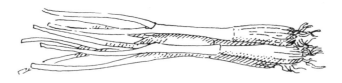

Cavolfiore, uvette sultanine, acciughe e pinoli con maccheroni

(Maccheroni with cauliflower, sultanas, anchovies and pine nuts) **

Cauliflower, calabrese, broccoli and purple sprouting broccoli appear a great deal in the pasta sauces of the south of Italy, and can be successfully interchanged to make use of whichever is in season. Sometimes the vegtable is actually cooked in the water with the pasta and sometimes it is cooked separately and added to the pasta with the sauce.

This recipe makes an excellent starter for any meal. I would not recommend it as a main course as its flavour is best appreciated in small quantities.

400 g (1 lb) maccheroni	*50 g (2 oz) sultanas soaked in*
1 small cauliflower	*warm water for 10 minutes and*
4 tbs olive oil	*dried in a tea towel*
1 onion, finely sliced	*50 g (2 oz) pine nuts*
1 tsp tomato purée	*4 tbs parmesan cheese*
a wine glass of water or stock	*a few leaves of basil*
4 anchovy fillets	

Divide the cauliflower into florets and simmer in boiling salted water until not quite tender. Gently heat 2 tablespoons of olive oil, add the finely sliced onion and cook over a low heat until transparent. Add the tomato purée and the water or stock and continue to cook until the sauce has reduced.

Add the cauliflower. Mash the anchovy fillets with a couple of tablespoons of olive oil until smooth. Add the anchovy paste, sultanas and pine nuts to the cauliflower and onion mixture and cook over a very low heat for 5 or 6 minutes to allow the flavours to blend.

Bring a large pan of salted water to the boil. Pour in the pasta and cook *al dente.*

Strain the pasta and transfer to a large serving dish. Add the sauce, the parmesan cheese and a few torn basil leaves. Stir well and serve at once.

Maccheroni con cimette di broccoli e mollica sfritta

(Maccheroni with calabrese and golden breadcrumbs) *

There are many variations on this recipe which make use of the excellent cauliflowers, broccoli and calabrese grown in the south of Italy. It also uses breadcrumbs in place of parmesan cheese, which is a reminder of the days when many people could not afford cheese. It is a simple dish that can be made in the time it takes to cook the pasta.

400 g (1 lb) maccheroni
200 g (8 oz) young calabrese heads
or cauliflower florets
800 g (2 lb) tinned plum tomatoes

4 tbs olive oil
50 g (2 oz) breadcrumbs, toasted
or fried in olive oil
salt to taste

Wash the calabrese and break the heads into small pieces. Strain the juice from the tomatoes and sieve them. Bring a large pan of salted water to the boil. Add the pasta and the calabrese and cook until the maccheroni is *al dente*.

Heat the olive oil in a pan. Add the sieved tomatoes and reduce them to a thick creamy consistency. Strain the pasta and calabrese and transfer to a large serving dish with 2 tablespoons of the cooking water. Add the tomato sauce and breadcrumbs, mix well and serve at once.

Emmenthal, carote e santoreggia con tagliatelle

(*Emmenthal, carrot, savory and tagliatelle*) **

250 g (10 oz) tagliatelle
1 tbs butter
100 g (4 oz) carrots
milk

salt and pepper
1 tbs fresh savory leaves, chopped
100 g (4 oz) emmenthal
parmesan cheese

Melt the butter in a small pan and add to it the carrots cut into matchstick strips. Stir over a low heat for 1 minute. Add enough milk to the pan to cover the carrots and a little salt and pepper to taste and cook over a medium heat until the carrots are firm but tender and most of the milk has evaporated. Add the chopped savory and mix in. Cut the emmenthal into strips of similar size to the carrots.

Bring a large pan of salted water to the boil. Pour in the pasta and cook *al dente*.

Strain the pasta and transfer to a large serving dish. Add the carrots, any remaining pan juices and the strips of cheese, stir well and serve at once. Add black pepper and parmesan to taste.

Spaghetti con zucchini, pinoli tostati e prezzemolo
(Spaghetti with courgettes, toasted pine nuts and parsley) **

Courgettes are easy to grow and are cheap and plentiful throughout the summer. In Italy they are generally harvested when they are only 8 cm (3 in) long which means they are young and tender and their texture is creamy. Here they are usually picked when they are past their best, as shape and size seem to be valued more than taste and texture. If you grow your own courgettes, pick them when they are really small.

In Italy they are most often eaten stuffed with meat or breadcrumbs, baked in the oven and served as a starter; or cut into slivers, dipped in a light batter, deep-fried and served as a vegetable. In the summer, the yellow lily-shaped courgette flowers are exquisite to eat as a starter, either plain or stuffed, dipped in batter and deep-fried.

This dish is an excellent way of serving courgettes when they are cheap and plentiful at the end of the summer. Their bright green colour contrasts wonderfully with the pasta. This is my variation on a traditional Sicilian dish and does not require parmesan cheese.

400 g (1 lb) spaghetti	*3 tbs olive oil*
1 handful of pine nuts	*salt and pepper to taste*
400 g (1 lb) young courgettes	*a few sprigs of parsley*
1 clove of garlic	

Toast the pine nuts under a hot grill until brown, taking care not to burn them. Slice the courgettes very thinly and chop the garlic finely with a *mezzaluna*. Heat the olive oil in a large frying pan or wok, add the garlic and turn once. Then add the courgettes and stir-fry over a medium heat until golden.

Bring a large pan of salted water to the boil. Pour in the pasta and cook *al dente*.

Strain the pasta, transfer to a large serving dish and add the courgettes, boiling hot oil and toasted pine nuts. Stir well, sprinkle with parsley and serve at once.

Funghi freschi, nepetella, aglio e limone con rigatoni
(Field mushrooms, catmint, garlic and lemon with rigatoni) **

If you walk in the countryside in autumn it is always wise to go well prepared. Over and above the obvious raincoat and suitable footwear, slip a paper bag or two into your pocket as there is some legal poaching to be done! The prize which goes unseen by the majority of walkers is the field mushroom, still to be found in any pasture that is left for nature to tend. Unlike the blackberry that cascades profusely over the hedgerows for all who pass to see, the mushroom likes to hide itself away. So keep your eyes open, especially if you are out in the early morning, when mushrooms are at their freshest.

This recipe is based on a Tuscan way of preparing porcini or ovoli mushrooms, which are not easy to come by unless dried. I therefore like to use freshly gathered field mushrooms which have a distinctive flavour and something of the fleshy texture of their more exotic Italian relations.

400 g (1 lb) rigatoni or spaghetti	salt and pepper to taste
400 g (1 lb) field mushrooms	½ tbs tomato purée
1 small wine glass of olive oil	1 cup of stock or hot water
3 cloves of garlic	a large knob of butter
a bunch of catmint or parsley	2 tbs parmesan cheese, freshly
2 tbs lemon juice	grated

Wash the mushrooms thoroughly, pat them dry and slice them very thinly. Heat the olive oil, garlic and catmint very gently until the garlic turns golden. Discard the catmint and the garlic and add the sliced mushrooms to the oil. Cook over a very low heat, turning them carefully until they have absorbed the olive oil. Add the lemon juice and salt and pepper to taste, then cover and cook for 10 minutes.

Dissolve the tomato purée in a cupful of stock or hot water and add a little at a time, to prevent the mushrooms from drying out. Cook for a further 10 minutes.

Bring a large pan of salted water to the boil. Pour in the pasta and cook *al dente*.

Strain the pasta and transfer to a large serving dish. Add the butter, the parmesan cheese and half the mushrooms. Stir well. Serve at once with an extra spoonful of mushrooms on each plate.

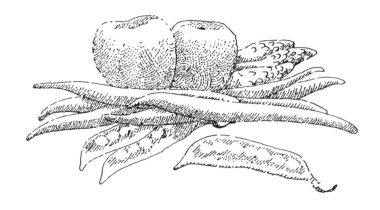

Fagiolini, asparagi e piselli dolci con trenette

(Trenette with French beans, asparagus and mangetout) **

400 g (1 lb) trenette (very thin tagliatelle)
100 g (4 oz) French beans
100 g (4 oz) mangetout
8 asparagus spears
50 g (2 oz) butter

salt and pepper
3 or 4 plum tomatoes drained, deseeded and chopped
2 tbs freshly grated parmesan cheese

Top and tail the French beans and the mangetout. Cut the tender part of the asparagus into 2 cm (1 in) pieces and discard any tough parts. Cut the beans in half. Melt the butter in a heavy-based pan. Add the vegetables and a little salt to taste and cook over a low heat for 2 or 3 minutes. Add the chopped tomatoes, cover the pan and continue cooking for 5 minutes until the vegetables are firm but tender.

Bring a large pan of salted water to the boil. Pour in the pasta and cook *al dente*.

Strain the pasta and transfer to a large serving dish. Add the vegetables, a grinding of black pepper and the parmesan cheese, stir well and serve at once.

Spaghetti spezzati con porri e pancetta
(Snapped spaghetti with leeks and bacon) **

A tasty, warming, winter pasta dish, easy to make for a simple supper yet special enough for a party starter. For the vegetarian, omit the bacon and cook the leeks in melted butter, adding a carton of single cream when tender and warming the mixture through before adding it to the pasta.

400 g (1 lb) pasta	½ tsp mustard powder
4 medium-sized leeks	salt and pepper
200 g (8 oz) bacon or 250 ml	freshly grated parmesan cheese
(½ pint) single cream	

Cut away and discard the tough dark green part of the leeks. Cut the rest into 4 cm (1½ in) pieces, and again into matchstick slivers. Wash in plenty of running water, blanch in boiling water and dry thoroughly in a salad spinner or towel.

Chop the bacon into small cubes and stir-fry over a medium to high heat in its own fat until crisp. Add the leek strips, stir-fry until tender but firm, add the mustard powder and mix well.

Bring a large pan of salted water to the boil. Break the pasta into 5 cm (2 in) lengths. Pour in the pasta and cook *al dente*.

Strain the pasta into a large serving dish, add the leeks, bacon, pan juices and parmesan, stir well and serve at once.

Spaghetti con peperonata
(Spaghetti with pepper stew) **

Pasta served with peppers is a typical dish all over southern Italy and Sicily where vegetables grow to perfection. My peperonata recipe was given to me many years ago by Antonia Mazzanti, but I confess it never tastes as good as hers did. Peppers do not have the same sweetness, flavour and succulence here that they have in Italy. Avoid green peppers as they are bitter.

400 g (1 lb) spaghetti	peppers
2 large sweet onions	400 g (1 lb) tinned plum tomatoes,
4 tbs good olive oil	drained and deseeded
a handful of parsley	more parsley to garnish
2 large yellow and 2 large red	

Peel and thinly slice the onions and chop the parsley. Gently heat the olive oil in a large saucepan, add the onions and the parsley and cook over a low heat until really tender, at least 20 minutes.

Blanch the peppers for 1 minute in boiling water. Lift them out and allow to cool a little. Cut them in half, peel away the thin skin and remove the seeds. Cut the peppers into strips, add them to the onion and cook over a gentle heat for 10 minutes.

Cut the tomatoes into strips, pat them dry, add them to the peppers and onions and stir carefully. Cover and cook over a very low heat for at least 30 minutes or until tender. Shake the pan occasionally to prevent sticking.

Bring a large pan of salted water to the boil. Pour in the pasta and cook *al dente*.

Strain the pasta and transfer to a large serving dish. Add the peperonata and 2 tablespoons of pasta water, stir well and serve at once, sprinkled with chopped parsley.

Fettutine al Geo

(Fettucine with mushrooms, cream and Marsala wine) **

Of all the pasta dishes that la Signora Monetti used to make this was probably my favourite. It was one of the first pasta dishes I cooked for my friends when I came home from Italy. The sauce is delicious served with steak, veal and pork as well as pasta.

250 g (10 oz) light fettucine	*half a glass of Marsala wine or*
50 g (2 oz) butter	*2 tbs sweet sherry*
1 clove of garlic, crushed	*salt and pepper*
a handful of parsley, chopped	*125 ml (¼ pint) stock or water*
250 g (10 oz) button mushrooms,	*250 ml (½ pint) single cream*
thinly sliced	*2 tbs freshly grated parmesan*

Melt the butter in a large heavy-based frying pan. Add the garlic, parsley and mushrooms and allow them to cook gently over a low heat, stirring from time to time.

When the butter has been absorbed and the mushrooms start to soften, add the Marsala wine, salt to taste and a grinding of black pepper, and stir. Cover and allow to cook over a very low heat for 30 minutes. Add a little of the warm stock or water every now and then to prevent the mushrooms from drying out. Add the cream at the last minute and heat through gently so that it is hot at the time that the pasta is cooked.

Bring a large pan of salted water to the boil. Pour in the pasta and cook *al dente*.

Strain the pasta and transfer to a large serving dish. Add the mushrooms and cream, 2 tablespoons of pasta water and the freshly grated parmesan. Stir well and serve at once.

PASTA E FORMAGGIO

Parmesan plus

Italy produces a vast assortment of cheeses. Many of them are well known in Britain, such as parmesan, gorgonzola, mozzarella, bel paese and dolcelatte. Among the less well known are provelone, pecorino, stracchino, caciocavallo, caciotta, fontina, mascarpone and ricotta. There are also countless country cheeses that are local and in some cases seasonal, like morlacco from the hills of Asolo (north of Venice), which is only available in June, July and August. These are rarely seen outside the area of production, never mind outside Italy.

Most pasta dishes with the exception of the fish ones would be incomplete without cheese, as is reflected in the Italian proverb *Cascare come cacio sui maccheroni* (to fall like cheese on maccheroni).

Parmesan is not the only cheese served with pasta. Other types of hard cheese such as pecorino and caciocavallo are used. Besides being excellent by themselves, most Italian cheeses make delicious dressings for pasta, either melted with cream or cut into splinters and stirred into the pasta with other ingredients.

Borragine, mascarpone e pinoli tostati
(Borage, Italian cream cheese and toasted pine nuts) *

This is a simple and unusual sauce. The contrasts in texture and flavour of the rich cream cheese, the refreshing borage leaves and the aromatic toasted pine nuts make it an interesting starter, and a pretty one if served in summer decorated with the vivid blue star-like borage flowers. It takes minutes to prepare and is substantial enough to serve as a simple supper dish for friends.

250 g (10 oz) tagliatelle	*salt and black pepper*
200 g (8 oz) mascarpone, or 2	*1 handful of young borage leaves,*
parts cream cheese and 1 part	*finely chopped*
lightly whipped double cream (see	*2 tbs toasted pine nuts*
page 115)	*12 borage flowers*
50 g (2 oz) butter	

Bring a large pan of salted water to the boil. Pour in the pasta and cook *al dente*.

Gently heat the mascarpone and butter and add a little salt, a grinding of black pepper and a spoonful of the chopped borage. Stir and allow to stand. Toast the pine nuts either under the grill or in the oven on medium heat. Take care not to burn them.

Strain the pasta and transfer to a large serving dish. Add the mascarpone, the pine nuts and the rest of the chopped borage leaves, stir well and serve at once. Float the borage flowers in a shallow dish of water and scatter two or three of them on each serving of pasta.

Penne al mascarpone, spinaci e bacon
(Pasta quills with mascarpone, spinach and crispy bacon) **

400 g (1 lb) quills or short pasta	*2 parts cream cheese and 1 part*
150 g (6 oz) young spinach leaves	*lightly whipped double cream*
150 g (6 oz) bacon	*(see page 115)*
1 clove of garlic, crushed	*black pepper*
200 g (8 oz) mascarpone, or	*parmesan cheese*

Wash and dry the spinach leaves very carefully and tear them into bite-size pieces. Chop the bacon into small pieces and fry with the garlic until the fat runs and the bacon becomes crispy.

Bring a large pan of salted water to the boil. Pour in the pasta and cook *al dente*.

Warm the mascarpone cheese very gently and dilute it with 4 table-spoons of water from the pasta pan.

Strain the pasta and transfer to a large serving dish. Add the mascarpone and a grinding of black pepper and stir well. Add the spinach leaves and the bacon and bacon fat, stir again and serve at once with freshly grated parmesan cheese.

Farfalle ai quattro formaggi
(Pasta bows with four cheeses) *

A mixture of any four cheeses can be used provided that they are of varying character, making this a useful way of finishing the bits of cheese left over from a party cheeseboard. I like to use dolcelatte, which is off-white in colour with blue-green veins and has a strong flavour and a creamy moist texture.

400 g (1 lb) pasta bows
50 g (2 oz) mozzarella
50 g (2 oz) emmenthal
50 g (2 oz) fresh parmesan

50 g (2 oz) butter
50 g (2 oz) dolcelatte
salt

Bring a large pan of salted water to the boil. Pour in the pasta and cook *al dente*.

Chop the mozzarella into small cubes, roughly grate the emmenthal and cut the parmesan into slivers. Put the butter and the dolcelatte into a basin and melt it either in a microwave oven or over a pan of boiling water.

Strain the pasta and transfer to a large serving dish. Add the cheeses and butter together with a grating of nutmeg and stir well until all the cheeses are mixed in and start to melt. Serve at once.

93

Gorgonzola con crema, prezzemolo e penne rigate
(Gorgonzola, cream and parsley with ridged quills) *

Gorgonzola is a fairly strong but creamy blue cheese made from cows' milk in Lombardy, the region around Milan. Originally the curd was left to stand in damp caves to form natural mould but today penicillin and copper wires are introduced to the cheese to speed up the process. It takes about six months for a cheese to mature.

400 g (1 lb) pasta quills	100 g (4 oz) gorgonzola
50 g (2 oz) butter	a large bunch of parsley
250 ml (½ pint) single cream	salt and pepper

Bring a large pan of salted water to the boil. Pour in the pasta and cook *al dente*.

Heat the butter and cream together over a low heat. Cut the gorgonzola into very small cubes and roughly chop the parsley.

Strain the pasta and transfer to a large serving dish. Add the gorgonzola, cream, a grinding of black pepper and half the parsley. Stir well, sprinkle with the remaining parsley and serve at once.

Farfalle con lattuga, prosciutto cotto, fiocchi di emmenthal e noce moscato
(Pasta bows with lettuce, ham and emmenthal) *

A simple and flavoursome yet interesting pasta starter for a summer supper party. This is an ideal way of using up a tired lettuce and the end of a piece of cooked ham. Please try it, because it really is delicious.

400 g (1 lb) pasta bows	2½ cm (1 in) slivers
25 g (1 oz) butter	125 ml (5 fl oz) carton single
1 small onion	cream
150 g (6 oz) iceberg lettuce	50 g (2 oz) emmenthal cheese, cut
a grating of nutmeg	into 2½ cm (1 in) slivers
100 g (4 oz) cooked ham, cut into	salt

Chop the onion finely. Melt the butter in a heavy-based pan (a large wok is ideal). Add the onion and fry over a low heat until transparent. Cut the lettuce into shreds and add to the onion. Add a grating of nutmeg and stir-fry for 5 minutes until the lettuce starts to soften. Add the ham and the cream and heat through gently.

Bring a large pan of salted water to the boil. Add the pasta and cook *al dente.*

Strain the pasta and transfer to a large serving dish. Add the cooked lettuce and ham and the cheese slivers and stir well. Serve at once.

Tagliatelle con pistacchi e dolcelatte
(Tagliatelle with pistachio nuts and dolcelatte) *

This is a very rich pasta sauce and is best served as a starter. It is a useful way of using up any type of blue cheese that may be past its best. Stilton, for example, is ideal.

250 g (10 oz) tagliatelle	*250 ml (½ pint) single cream*
50 g (2 oz) grated dolcelatte or	*pepper and salt*
other blue cheese	*50 g (2 oz) shelled pistachio nuts,*
50 g (2 oz) butter	*roughly chopped*

Boil a large pan of water. When it reaches a rolling boil add a handful of coarse salt and the pasta and cook *al dente.*

Carefully melt the cheese with the butter and cream over a low heat or in the microwave. Add a grinding of black pepper. Have the chopped pistachios at the ready.

When the pasta is cooked, strain it and transfer it to a large serving dish. Add the cream and cheese sauce, 2 tablespoons of pasta water and half the pistachio nuts. Stir well and serve at once sprinkled with the remaining chopped nuts.

Ruote al pomodoro, mozzarella e capperi
(Pasta wheels pizza style) **

I love the combination of creamy tomato sauce, strands of melted mozzarella and juicy capers.

400 g (1 lb) pasta wheels	*300 g (12 oz) mozzarella, thinly*
a double quantity of tomato sauce	*sliced*
(see page 24)	*olive oil*
1 or 2 tbs capers	*oregano*

Make a double quantity of tomato sauce.

Preheat the oven to 200°C (400°F, gas 6).

Bring a large pan of salted water to the boil. Pour in the pasta and cook *al dente*. Strain the pasta and return to the pan. Add the tomato sauce and most of the capers, stir well and pour into a greased shallow ovenproof dish.

Cover with thin slices of mozzarella and scatter a few capers on top; sprinkle with a little olive oil and some oregano and place in the oven for 10 minutes or until the cheese has melted. Serve at once.

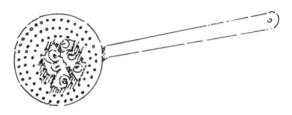

PASTA PARTICOLARE
Party pasta

Spaghetti con carciofi, piselli e prosciutto crudo
(Spaghetti with artichokes, peas and Parma ham) ✲✲ ●

This is a great dish to serve in the summer when artichokes and peas are in season. Both Parma ham and artichokes are expensive, so I like to serve it as a starter for a very special meal. It can be made using canned artichokes and bacon for an elegant and simple storecupboard starter.

400 g (1 lb) spaghetti	1 small onion
750 g (1¾ lb) fresh peas in pods	50 g (2 oz) Parma ham or bacon
or 150 g (6 oz) frozen peas	3 tbs olive oil
4 globe artichokes or 8 canned	half a glass of stock or white wine
artichoke hearts*	and water
lemon juice	salt and pepper

If using fresh vegetables, shell the peas. Clean the fresh artichokes by removing the outer, tougher leaves, cut them into quarters and immerse them in cold water and lemon juice. Finely chop the onion and Parma ham. Place them in a heavy-based pan with the olive oil and cook gently over a low heat until transparent. Add the artichokes and fry until they start to change colour. Add the peas, cover with stock and simmer gently for 20 minutes.

* Note: cut the tinned artichokes into four and dry well on absorbent paper. Soak them for half an hour in milk and dry again. This removes the harsh briny taste.

If fresh vegetables are not being used, simply add the tinned artichoke hearts to the fried onion and bacon and cook for a few minutes to absorb the oil. Then add the peas and half the quantity of stock and simmer for 10 minutes. Season to taste.

Bring a large pan of salted water to the boil. Pour in the pasta and cook *al dente*.

Strain the pasta and transfer to a large serving dish. Add the artichokes, peas and Parma ham, stir well and serve at once.

Pasticcio di rigatoni, fegatini, funghi secchi, specie e porto
(Chicken liver, mushroom and rigatoni tart) ✱✱✱

A *pasticcio* is a traditional dish from Emilia Romagna. It is a covered pie, made with a slightly sweet shortcrust pastry and filled with pasta dressed with béchamel, tomato or meat sauce. Elsewhere in Italy this kind of pie is called *una torta di pasta*, a pasta tart, and a *pasticcio* is a kind of unruly lasagne, using the word *pasticcio* more in its colloquial sense, a 'mess'!

The double meaning of *pasticcio* holds a particularly fond memory for me. The very first Italian cookery book I owned (Pellegrino Artusi's *La Scienza in Cucina e l'Arte di Mangiar Bene*) was given to me by two of my Bolognese friends when they came to visit me in Rome. They inscribed the book with the words *'Con la speranza che tu migliori i tuoi "pasticci" culinari'* Roma 20–7–1970. ('In the hope that you improve your culinary messes . . . or did they mean pies?)

This is a filling dish involving worthwhile but lengthy preparation. It is ideal for a winter lunch or supper party or a special family meal. You can substitute your family's favourite meat sauce for the chicken liver sauce.

Pastry

400 g (1 lb) plain flour	*half a lemon*
50 g (2 oz) icing sugar	*200 g (8 oz) soft unsalted butter*
salt	*4 egg yolks*

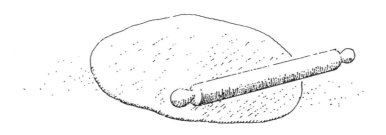

Filling

400 g (1 lb) rigatoni	*tomatoes drained, deseeded and*
200 g (½ lb) chicken livers	*chopped (reserve the juice)*
50 g (2 oz) butter	*pinch each of cinnamon and mixed*
25 g (1 oz) dried mushrooms,	*spice*
soaked and dried (see page 114)	*salt and pepper*
3 tbs port wine	*4 tbs freshly grated parmesan*
400 g (1 lb) tinned plum	*cheese*

Sieve the flour, a pinch of salt and the sugar. Make a well, add the grated zest of the lemon, the butter cut into slivers, a few drops of lemon juice and the egg yolks. Work quickly into a ball and knead. Wrap in greaseproof paper and leave to stand in the refrigerator for at least an hour.

Wash and dry the chicken livers. Melt 50 g (2 oz) of butter in a frying pan, add the chopped chicken livers and the softened mushrooms and fry over a medium heat for 5 minutes. Add the port to the pan and cook for a further 5 minutes. Reduce the heat and add the tomatoes. Add the cinnamon, spice and salt, stir well and continue to cook for 15 minutes. If the sauce starts to dry out too much, add a little of the reserved tomato juice.

Preheat the oven to 180°C (350°F, gas 4). Butter a large baking tray. Roll out the pastry into two circles of unequal size, allowing one third for the base and two thirds for the top.

Bring a large pan of salted water to the boil. Pour in the pasta and cook for half the required cooking time. Strain the pasta and transfer to a large dish, add the chicken liver sauce and the parmesan cheese and stir well.

Lay the smaller circle of pastry on the baking tray and pile the pasta in the middle, leaving a border all the way round. Cover with the second circle of pastry to form a 'dome'. Seal the edges with egg yolk and trim. With the trimmings make pastry 'ribbons' and a 'bow', which can be used to tie up the 'parcel'. Paint the parcel with egg yolk.

Place in the oven for 45 minutes, stand for 10 minutes and serve.

Timballo di fettucine, granchio e gamberi
(Crab and prawn pasta ring) ***

Crab arrives on my local fish stall already boiled, so I can simply take it home and get the hammer out! It is hard work cleaning a crab. I prepare the body and the two big claws and let the guests get to work on the rest at the table! The white meat from the claws is flaky, crisp and moist, while the dark meat scooped from the body is excellent for patés and fish sauces as it has a creamy texture and a strong flavour.

This dish is fiddly, but it makes an attractive and delicious hot buffet dish or main course for a summer supper party. Serve it with a green salad.

The pasta and custard can be prepared beforehand, poured into the ring mould and set aside until required. The sauce too can be made beforehand and heated when required. These quantities should be enough for a starter for 12 or a main course for 6 or 8. Use a 3 litre (6 pint) ring mould.

500 g (1¼ lb) tagliatelle
salt

Sauce

100 g (4 oz) brown crab meat
100 g (4 oz) chopped prawns
375 ml (nearly 1 pint) single cream

Custard

100 g (4 oz) brown or brown and
white crab meat
100 g (4 oz) chopped prawns
375 ml (almost 1 pint) single

cream
3 egg yolks
50 g (2 oz) parmesan
50 g (2 oz) butter

To finish

butter
toasted breadcrumbs
200 g (8 oz) whole prawns and small crab claws to garnish

Pound all the brown crab meat until smooth and creamy. Add all the chopped prawns and cream, mix well and divide between two bowls. To half the crab and prawns add the egg yolks, parmesan cheese and butter. This is the custard. The remaining crab and prawn mixture will be heated and served with the pasta at the table.

Preheat the oven to 180°C (350°F, gas 4).

Bring a large pan of salted water to the boil. Pour in the pasta and cook until slightly undercooked. When the pasta is ready, strain it and transfer it to a large mixing bowl. Add the prawn and crab custard and mix well.

Butter a large ring mould and coat it with the toasted breadcrumbs. Pour the pasta into the mould, shake well to settle it, sprinkle with breadcrumbs and dot with butter. Place the ring mould in a *bain marie*. Cook in the oven for 20 minutes (30 minutes if the mould was prepared in advance).

Toss the prawns in melted butter and lay them out on a flat dish in the oven to brown. Warm the sauce through, either in a microwave or over a low heat. Remove the pasta ring from the oven and allow it to stand for 5 minutes before turning it out onto a serving dish. Decorate with the whole prawns and small crab claws. Cut the ring into slices and spoon a little of the sauce over each serving.

Anatra arrosto con salsa Bolognese e pappardelle
(Roast duck in orange and Marsala wine sauce with pappardelle) ** *

Wild duck is one of the traditional game meats of Emilia Romagna, the Veneto and other northern regions of Italy, prepared by cutting the duck into small pieces, browning them with a *battuto* of belly pork and onion and then cooking them slowly with white wine, carrot and celery until tender. The sauce is then served with tagliatelle as a starter and the duck as a main course with a few vegetables.

In this recipe, duck leftovers are served with pasta in a 'Bolognese' sauce, which many may be surprised to learn is traditionally an orange sauce served with either boiled, roast or grilled meat!

400 g (1 lb) pappardelle (wide tagliatelle)
100 g (4 oz) butter
1 tbs cornflour
half a wine glass of dry Marsala wine
half a wine glass of water
the juice and the zest of 1 small orange

1 tsp icing sugar
250 ml (½ pint) single cream or left-over duck sauce
150 g (6 oz) duck carcass pickings (cut into small strips)
2 tbs breadcrumbs fried in a little butter
salt and pepper

Melt the butter in a small pan. Add the flour and stir well with a wooden spoon. When the roux is smooth add the Marsala wine and water and continue mixing over a low heat until the sauce thickens. Add the orange juice and sugar, the zest cut into matchstick strips, the cream and the strips of duck meat. Heat through thoroughly, stirring all the while.

Meanwhile bring a large pan of salted water to the boil. Pour in the pasta and cook *al dente*.

Strain the pasta and transfer to a large serving dish. Add the sauce, the breadcrumbs and a grinding of black pepper, stir well and serve at once.

Crostata di pasta, champignons e farfalle
(Flaky pastry case filled with 'buttons and bows') ✳✳✳

Tortellini, ravioli and various kinds of short pasta tossed in a rich white sauce flavoured with cheese, prawns and mushrooms can be served in a warm, pre-cooked flaky pastry case.

200 g (8 oz) pack flaky pastry	*fresh coriander*
a little milk	*salt*
50 g (2 oz) butter	*béchamel sauce (see page 23)*
200 g (8 oz) button mushrooms	*300 g (12 oz) pasta bows*
1 packet or small bunch of	*2 tbs freshly grated parmesan*

Preheat the oven to 190°C (375°F, gas 5).

Roll out the flaky pastry and cover the *outside* of an upside-down overproof flan dish 20 cm (8 in) in diameter. (It should first be greased and lightly brushed with water.) Trim off the excess pastry with a serrated pastry wheel to give the flan case a decorated edge. Place the dish and the pastry (still upside down) on a greased baking tray. Make holes all over the pastry with a fork, brush with milk and place in the oven for 20 minutes.

Melt 50 g (2 oz) of butter in a large frying pan. Slice the mushrooms finely, add them to the butter and cook over a very low heat. When they have absorbed the butter add half the coriander, chopped finely, and a little salt, then cover and cook for a further 20 minutes. If they start to dry out add a little stock or water.

Pour the pasta into boiling water and cook *al dente*.

Make the béchamel sauce. Pour the white sauce on to the cooked mushrooms and stir well.

Strain the pasta and return to the pan, retaining a tablespoon of the pasta water. Mix in the mushroom sauce, the freshly grated parmesan and a grinding of black pepper. Remove the pastry case carefully from its mould and place it the right way up on a serving plate. Pile the pasta and mushroom sauce into the mould and garnish with sprigs of fresh coriander. Serve at once.

Tagliatelle con coscie di ranocchi
(Frogs' legs with tagliatelle) ✳✳

This pasta sauce is actually based on a traditional risotto recipe from southern Piedmont, recorded in Pellegrino Artusi's book.

400 g (1 lb) spaghetti
a bunch of parsley
1 clove of garlic
1 carrot
1 stick of celery
1 small onion

12 pairs of frogs' legs
2 tbs olive oil
50 g (2 oz) butter
2 tbs white wine
salt and pepper
parmesan cheese, freshly grated

Wash and finely chop half the parsley together with the garlic and vegetables. Wash and skin the frogs' legs and remove the bones. Put the olive oil and butter in a frying pan and warm it through over a low heat. Add the vegetables to the pan and cook over a low heat until transparent. Add the frogs' legs to the pan and stir well. Add the white wine to the pan, then cover and cook for 15 minutes. Stir frequently, adding a little water if necessary to prevent sticking.

Bring a large pan of salted water to the boil. Pour in the pasta and cook *al dente*.

Strain the pasta and transfer to a large serving dish. Add the frogs' leg sauce, the parmesan cheese and the remaining parsley, finely chopped. Stir well and serve at once.

Fazzoletti alle cape sante con panna e vino bianco
(Scallops served with pasta kerchiefs) ***

Fazzoletti (kerchiefs) are simply 10 cm (4 in) squares of pasta served sandwiched around a rich sauce. As far as I know they are a modern invention – I never came across them when I lived in Italy. They are a splendid innovation as a starter for a special meal because they do not involve much preparation, are not too filling and are an attractive and unusual way of serving a special sauce. Any cream-based sauce would be suitable to serve this way. The sauce in this recipe is also excellent with thin tagliatelle.

16 pasta kerchiefs (see below)
500 g (1¼ lb) fresh scallops
lemon juice
250 ml (½ pint) single cream
a pinch of mace
2 tbs spring onion tops, chopped

12 g (½ oz) butter
half a glass of white wine or
2 tbs dry vermouth
a little parsley
salt and pepper

Cut 16 10 cm (4 in) square pasta kerchiefs from a fresh *sfoglia* (see page 15) or take 8 sheets of ready-made lasagna pasta.

Wash the scallops thoroughly and remove the dark membrane and the small white opaque part at the side of the scallop. Pull off the coral and cut away and discard the brownish end. Cut the scallops horizontally into three rounds and cut each of these into quarters. Liquidize or sieve the corals and add the cream, mace, spring onion tops and a grinding of black pepper.

Melt a little butter in a frying pan and fry the scallops for a couple of minutes until golden, then add the white wine or vermouth, sprinkle with salt and a little lemon juice and simmer for three minutes. Pour the coral mixture into the pan and heat through very gently until just warm.

Slide half the sheets of pasta, one at a time, into plenty of boiling, salted water. Cook *al dente*: fresh pasta will only need two or three minutes whereas dried lasagne will need about 8 minutes (check the manufacturer's instructions). Remove with a slotted spoon as they come to the surface and place on a clean dry towel. Slide in the remaining pasta and repeat the process.

Meanwhile place a kerchief on each plate (if using lasagne cut each sheet of pasta into two), place a tablespoon of the scallop sauce on to each one and cover with a second kerchief as they are removed from the water. Place a small sprig of parsley on each sandwich and sprinkle with mace. Serve at once.

Pasta e arrosto

(Pasta and roast meat) ∗∗ ✳

In the north of Italy pasta is always served as a starter with just a coating of sauce, but from Naples down it is not unusual to serve pasta with a substantial casserole or roast. This might explain the British habit of serving large quantities of meat sauce with spaghetti. Most of the Italian immigrants and prisoners of war who have settled in Britain came from the south. Perhaps our spaghetti bolognese would be better called spaghetti neapolitan!

This recipe is based on a Calabrese dish from Anna Gosetti della Salda's book *Le Ricette Regionali Italiane*. It is a splendid and original way of serving any small game birds for a special meal.

300 g (12 oz) vermicelli or very thin spaghetti	*200 g (8 oz) pork*
4 quail	*olive oil*
rosemary	*salt and pepper*
sage	*red wine*

Preheat the oven to 170°C (325°F, gas 3).

Clean the quail and place small sprigs of rosemary and sage inside each one. Place the pork and the quail in a small roasting dish with the olive oil.

Add salt and pepper to taste. Place in the oven, basting with red wine from time to time, until the meat is tender (approximately 1 hour or a little less).

Bring a large pan of salted water to the boil. Pour in the pasta and cook *al dente*.

Remove the quail from the roasting pan and return them to the oven to keep warm. Chop the pork finely and add it to the pan juices. Stir well and reheat adding a little of the pasta water if necessary.

Strain the pasta and transfer to a large serving dish. Add the sauce and mix well. Serve with a quail and a sprig of fresh rosemary on each plate.

Faraona con farfalle
(Guinea fowl and pasta bows) ** *

Clean the birds. Place two sprigs of sage and two whole cloves of garlic inside each one. Cover the breast with rashers of bacon, wrap in foil and roast in the oven for 1 hour at 180°C (350°F, gas 4). With any left-over meat prepare the following sauce.

400 g (1 lb) pasta bows	soaked and dried (see page 114)
1 onion	half a glass of red wine
1 carrot	1 bay leaf
1 stick of celery	150 g (6 oz) cooked guinea fowl
a handful of parsley	meat
50 g (2 oz) butter	2 tbs parmesan cheese, freshly
20 g (1 oz) dried mushrooms,	grated

Chop the onion, carrot, celery and parsley together very finely. Melt the butter in a heavy-based pan. Add the vegetables and cook over a low heat until transparent. Add the treated mushrooms to the pan, then add the red wine and the bay leaf and cook for 10 minutes. Chop the meat into small pieces. Add to the vegetables and heat through.

Bring a large pan of salted water to the boil. Pour in the pasta and cook *al dente*.

Strain the pasta and transfer to a large serving dish. Add the guinea fowl mixture and parmesan, stir well and serve at once.

Rasagnole al fagiano con crema e cognac
(Pheasant with cream and cognac served with rasagnole) ** *

This is a fabulous way of cooking pheasant so don't use it only as a pasta sauce. Cook a brace of pheasant this way leaving out the cream and make a traditional gravy with the pan juices. The left-over meat can then be chopped up with a little sauce enriched with cream and cognac and served the following day with pasta.

400 g (1 lb) rasagnole or tagliatelle
1 pheasant
salt and pepper
250 g (8 oz) thinly-sliced streaky bacon
a few sprigs of rosemary
4 tbs olive oil
3 cloves of garlic

2 sprigs of sage
2 tbs brandy
1 glass of red wine
a little stock
375 ml (¾ pint) single cream
3 tbs freshly grated parmesan
parsley to garnish

Wash the pheasant and dry carefully. Sprinkle with salt and pepper and wrap the birds completely in the slices of bacon. Tuck sprigs of rosemary inside the bacon and secure with raffia or thin string.

Meanwhile heat the olive oil in a wide-based frying pan or wok and add the garlic and sage to the oil. When the garlic starts to sizzle add the bird to the pan, turning until brown all over. Add the brandy to the pan and cook until evaporated. Add the red wine and continue to cook with the lid on over a low heat until the bird has cooked through (about 90 minutes). Add a little stock to the pan from time to time if the sauce dries out too much.

When ready, remove the pheasant from the pan, discard the string and the bacon, joint the bird and remove the flesh from the bones. Arrange on a serving dish and keep warm. Remove the sage and garlic from the pan, add the cream to the pan juices and stir well.

Bring a large pan of salted water to the boil. Pour in the pasta and cook *al dente*.

Strain the pasta into a large serving dish. Add the sauce and parmesan, stir well and serve at once with a few pieces of pheasant on each serving of tagliatelle.

Tagliolini al caviale
(Tagliolini with caviare) *

This very simple and elegant pasta recipe was passed on to me by Myrna, a Californian art restorer who acquired a taste for Italian food while living in Florence. The basis of the dish is *pasta in bianco*, simply pasta served in melted butter to which both exotic and simple flavours may be added: grated white truffle, the juice of a lemon, mashed anchovy, garlic, chopped walnuts, parmesan cheese, spices, cocoa or crushed poppy seeds, to name but a few.

Because of the subtle nature of this type of sauce it is best served with very fine pasta and in small quantities as a starter rather than as a main course.

250 g (10 oz) fresh tagliolini	a grating of nutmeg
80 g (3 oz) butter	1 small pot lumpfish or caviare
1 large lemon	a little finely chopped parsley

Melt the butter in a large dish and add the grated zest of the lemon plus a tablespoon of juice, a grating of fresh nutmeg and half the caviare.

Bring a large pan of salted water to the boil. Pour in the pasta and cook *al dente*.

Strain the pasta and add it to the butter and lemon juice, then add 2 tablespoons of the pasta water and stir well. Add the caviare, stir again and serve at once sprinkled with a little finely chopped parsley rather than cheese. Add a teaspoon of caviare to garnish each serving of pasta.

Lasagne all'aragosta e ricotta
(Lobster and ricotta lasagne) **

This is a dish for a grand occasion. Replace the lobster with fresh cod and some prawns and you have an equally delicious but inexpensive supper dish. Lasagne can be made with all kinds of fillings, not just the traditional meat and béchamel sauces. Try layers of mozzarella, ricotta or tomato sauce instead of white sauce, and mushrooms, aubergines, ratatouille or fish instead of meat. The meat sauce can be made with pork, lamb, poultry or game as well as with beef.

300 g (12 oz) lasagne	2 tbs parsley and thyme leaves,
one 1 kg (2–2½ lb) lobster, ready	finely chopped
cooked, or 400 g (1 lb) cod plus	100 g (4 oz) parmesan, finely
200 g (8 oz) shelled prawns	grated
béchamel sauce (see page 23)	butter
250 g (10 oz) ricotta	

Slide 4 or 6 sheets of lasagne into a pan of rapidly boiling salted water. When they are not quite tender, remove with a slotted spoon, plunge into cold water and allow to drain on a clean tea towel. Repeat the process until all the lasagne have been used up.

Remove the meat from the tail and claws of the lobster and chop up roughly.

Preheat the oven to 200°C (400°F, gas 6).

Make the béchamel sauce. Beat the ricotta into the béchamel sauce and add the parsley and thyme.

Butter a large roasting tin and cover the bottom with a layer of lasagne. Sprinkle with lobster and cover with a layer of sauce. Sprinkle with parmesan and repeat with the layers until all the ingredients have been used up. End with a layer of lasagne, which should be painted with melted butter and sprinkled with parmesan. Place in the oven for 20 to 30 minutes until brown.

Penne con pomodoro, mozzarella, prosciutto crudo e basilico

(Quills with tomato, mozzarella, Parma ham and basil) **

400 g (1 lb) pasta quills
1 quantity tomato sauce
(see page 24)
150 g (6 oz) mozzarella

100 g (4 oz) Parma ham
2 tbs parmesan cheese
8 basil leaves

Prepare the tomato sauce. Chop the mozzarella into small dice and the Parma ham into slivers.

Bring a large pan of salted water to the boil. Pour in the pasta and cook *al dente.*

Strain the pasta and transfer to a large serving dish. Add the tomato sauce, Parma ham and parmesan cheese and stir well. Add the mozzarella and stir well. Sprinkle with torn basil leaves and serve at once.

Tagliatelle con salmone affumicato, vodka e caviale

(Tagliatelle with smoked salmon, vodka and caviare) *

250 g (10 oz) tagliatelle
50 g (2 oz) butter
250 ml (½ pint) single cream
2 tbs vodka
black pepper

100 g (4 oz) smoked salmon pieces
2 tbs lumpfish caviare
1 tbs chopped dill, and some plumes to garnish

Bring a large pan of salted water to the boil. Pour in the pasta and cook *al dente.*

Melt the butter over a very low heat, add the cream and vodka and a grinding of black pepper and shake the pan from time to time as the sauce warms through. Cut the salmon into strips and have the lumpfish at the ready.

Strain the pasta and transfer to a large serving dish. Add the cream sauce and 2 tablespoons of pasta water and mix well. Add the lumpfish, the salmon and the chopped dill and stir again. Serve at once, decorating each serving with a small plume of dill.

Rotolo ripieno

(Italian roly-poly pasta) ***

As far as I know, nobody has yet managed to make a commercial *rotolo ripieno* and it is worth learning to make a *sfoglia* (see page 15) if only to be able to try one. As an alternative to this recipe, the roll can be filled with layers of meat sauce, spinach and sliced cooked mushrooms and served with a thin béchamel sauce.

This serves eight as a starter. Use a 3-egg *sfoglia* for a main course for eight and increase the other ingredients accordingly. Cut the dough in half and make two smaller *rotoli*.

Sfoglia

200 g (7 oz) plain flour
2 fresh eggs

Filling

1 kg (2 lb) spinach
salt and pepper
nutmeg to taste
1 tbs grated parmesan
200 g (8 oz) butter
400 g (1 lb) salmon

1 lemon
1 tbs chopped dill, plus a few sprigs
1 tbs chopped parsley, plus a few sprigs
200 g (8 oz) shelled prawns

Sauce

a wine glass of salmon stock
a wine glass of single cream
1 tbs chopped dill

To garnish

200 g (8 oz) whole prawns

Wash the spinach thoroughly in running water and then put it into a large pan with the water that is left on the leaves and a little salt. Simmer until tender. When the spinach is ready, strain and allow it to cool a little. Squeeze out the remaining water and chop it very finely with a sharp knife or *mezzaluna*. Add 75 g (3 oz) of the butter, salt, pepper, nutmeg to taste and a tablespoon of grated parmesan.

Lightly poach the salmon in a little water with a wedge of lemon and a few sprigs of fresh dill and parsley. Remove the salmon from the water as soon as the fish has set. Peel off the skin and take the salmon off the bone. Return the skin and bone to the cooking liquid and simmer, uncovered, over a low heat for 20 minutes or until reduced by half. Meanwhile flake the salmon with a fork, chop the prawns, and combine these with 50 g (2 oz) of softened butter and the chopped herbs. Mix well.

Make the *sfoglia* and roll it out. Cut it into a large rectangle approximately 50 cm by 30 cm (20 in by 12 in) and lay it out on a clean tea towel. Spread the spinach on the *sfoglia*, leaving a margin of 2 cm (1 in) all the way round. Then spread the fish mixture over the top of the spinach.

Roll up the *sfoglia* as you would a swiss roll and enclose the whole thing tightly in the cloth. Tie both ends securely and bind the roll so that it keeps its shape while it is being cooked (see diagram opposite). The roll can be stored in the fridge at this stage for several hours and cooked when required.

Take a large basting tin and fill it with enough salted water to cover the roll. Bring the water to the boil, and gently immerse the roll. Simmer for 1 hour.

Preheat the oven to 220°C (425°F, gas 7).

Carefully lift the roll out of the pan with the help of a couple of fish slices. Remove the cloth and cut the roll into slices. Arrange the slices in a large, buttered, ovenproof dish. Melt the remaining butter. Place a whole prawn on each slice and pour the butter over them. Place the dish in the oven for 10 minutes.

Meanwhile strain the salmon stock, add to it the single cream and a tablespoon of chopped dill and heat through gently. Remove the *rotolo* slices from the oven and serve at once accompanied by the sauce.

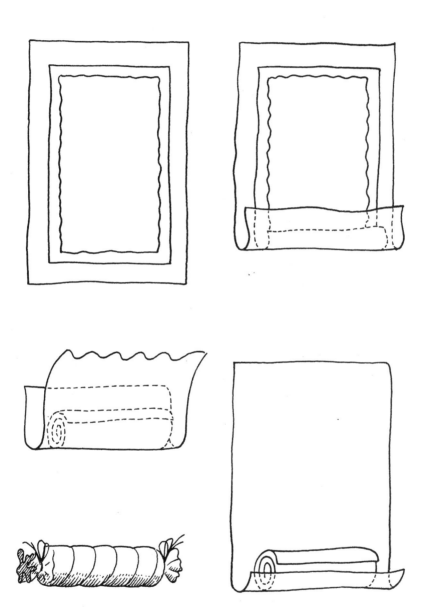

A PASTA COOK'S GLOSSARY

Al dente This is the Italian way of describing pasta when it is cooked to perfection (see *Cooking and Serving Perfect Pasta*, page 9).

Anchovy fillets They are used in many Italian dishes but their flavour can be overpowering; to tone down the saltiness soak them in milk for 30 minutes, rinse and pat dry before use.

Artusi, Pellegrino Florentine banker and failed literary writer. He compiled, at the turn of the century, the first cookery book to be aimed at the middle classes of the newly unified Italian nation. It was called *La Scienza in Cucina e l'Arte di Mangiar Bene* ('Science in the kitchen and the art of good eating'), and made him a household name with subsequent generations of Italians.

Artusi introduced to the Italian nation the habit of eating *pasta asciutta* (pasta served with sauce), suggesting that 'these pasta dishes would be suitable to alternate with the eternal and often tough and insipid boiled meat dishes.' Hitherto eating spaghetti with a tomato sauce was known only in Naples, tagliatelle with meat sauce only in Bologna and so on. It has been said that his cookery book was more effective in unifying the Italian people than anything written by the literary giants of the time.

Battuto Small quantities of two or three flavourings such as onion, carrot, celery, *pancetta*, garlic and herbs, chopped together finely and sweated before adding the principal ingredients of the sauce to the pan. Sometimes called *trito*.

Bavette The name given to narrow tagliatelle in southern Italy.

Bigoli The name given to spaghetti in the Veneto (the region around Venice). They are sometimes dyed black with squid ink.

Bucatini Long, spaghetti-like pasta with a channel running through the middle. They are popular in Italy, especially with ricotta and vegetable sauces, but sadly are seldom seen abroad.

Buon appetito means good appetite and is used at the beginning of every meal as the signal for everyone to dig in and enjoy their food.

Butter Traditionally, butter is used in the richer, pastoral areas of northern and central Italy, whereas olive oil is used for cooking in olive-growing regions, particularly southern Italy and Liguria. As a general guide, when cooking *pasta all'uovo* (tagliatelle and so on), use butter; when cooking other types, use olive oil.

Pasta served simply with butter and parmesan cheese is traditional 'invalid' food in Italy, popular with children and one of the best ways of savouring freshly made pasta. Finely chopped herbs and ground spices added to melted butter make excellent pasta dressings.

Cannelloni Rectangles of *pasta all'uovo*, stuffed and rolled.

Cannolicchi Short, straight, smooth maccheroni the width of the index finger, generally used in warming soups such as *pasta e fagioli* (pasta and red bean soup).

Capelli d'angelo (angel's hair) The narrowest spaghetti made, it is sold rolled up rather than dried straight and is served in consommé.

Cavatieddi Like orecchiette, a type of home-made pasta from Puglia (the heel of Italy), but shaped like little shells.

Chitarra, maccheroni alla A type of home-made egg pasta popular in the Abruzzo region. After being rolled and then cut into large rectangles, it is laid across and pressed through the *chitarra* or zither which cuts it into square threads. This pasta is served traditionally with a meat sauce made from lamb and peppers and also a tomato and chilli sauce.

Conchiglie Shell-shaped short pasta, small and large, ridged and smooth, good with rich fish sauces.

Condimento, condire *Condimento* means sauce, seasoning, flavouring or dressing and *condire* means to add sauce, to season, to flavour or to dress.

David, Elizabeth Author of a series of cookery books that inspired a generation of cooks to be adventurous. Her book on Italian food, written originally in 1954, is an excellent book of authentic Italian recipes and remains a classic.

Ditali (pasta thimbles) Short cuts of maccheroni.

Dried mushrooms Fresh porcini and other exotic mushrooms are dried and sold in small packets. Although they are expensive, a little goes a long way; 25 g (1 oz) of dried mushrooms is equivalent to 300 g (12 oz) of fresh. They must be soaked in warm milk for at least 30 minutes until completely soft.

Earthenware Many Italian dishes, according to tradition, should be cooked in earthenware pots.

Equipment There are three pieces of traditional kitchen equipment used for making hand made egg pasta. These are the *matterello*, an 80 cm (30 in) rolling pin, the *spianatoia*, a similarly proportioned board, and *la rotella dentata*, a serrated pastry wheel. These items have been used for pasta-making for at least 2500 years and are recorded pictorially in a famous Etruscan tomb, Grotta Bella, in a relief showing the interior of an Etruscan home of the fourth century BC.

Farfalle Pasta butterflies or bows, generally made from egg pasta.

Fettuccine The name given in Rome to tagliatelle. It is a diminutive of the word *fettuccia*, meaning ribbon.

Fusilli Short spaghetti spirals with a channel running through the centre.

Game Game figures a great deal in the regional cookery of Italy from Alto Adige in the north to Piemont in the west and from Friuli in the east down to Lazio as well as in the island of Sardinia, and to a certain extent in the south. The Italians serve game accompanied by a few artfully cooked vegetables, having used the pan juices to dress a plate of pasta as a starter. Delicious pasta sauces can be made from the leftovers (see pages 104–106).

Garlic (aglio) Garlic is not an essential ingredient in Italian cookery, but it is much used in the fish dishes and tomato-based sauces of the south. Northerners prefer a *battuto* of onions, celery, carrot and parsley as a basis for their dishes, but garlic does figure in the traditional pesto from Genoa and *bagna caöda* (a hot dip of walnut oil, anchovy and garlic for raw vegetables) and *agliata* (a sauce of walnuts, bread and garlic) from Piedmont. It is also used to enhance the flavour of many vegetable dishes. A delicious oil and garlic dressing for pasta can be made by following the recipe for *spaghetti all'arrabbiata* (see page 26), substituting plenty of garlic for the chilli.

Gnocchi Small dumplings made with potato or semolina. The g is silent – nyoki.

Grana A class of hard cheeses, to which parmesan belongs.

Gratinata Pasta served in a rich sauce, covered in breadcrumbs and put in the oven or under the grill to brown. Pasta is often served this way in Italy at the family table.

Lasagne Rectangular sheets of egg pasta used to make many traditional Italian oven-cooked pasta dishes. Sometimes coloured green by the addition of spinach (lasagne verdi).

Linguine Rather narrow tagliatelle, less than ½ cm (¼ in) wide. Also known as tagliolini, trenette and bavette.

Maccheroni (macaroni) Long or short pasta tubes, generally smooth but sometimes ridged.

Maltagliati Rhomboid shapes of home-made egg pasta.

Mascarpone A very rich, creamy soft cheese with a high fat content. Ordinary cream cheese can be used as a substitute for mascarpone in pasta sauces and puddings; beat together 1 part cheese with 1 part single cream, or 2 parts cheese with 1 part lightly whipped double cream. Many supermarkets now sell long-life mascarpone marketed by Polenghi, which is excellent.

Mezzaluna A two-handled knife with a curved blade; its rocking motion is traditionally used to chop the *battuto* finely. A food processor can be used instead for large quantities.

Millerighe Scored tubes of dried pasta; the name means 'a thousand lines'. Mezze maniche (short sleeves) are half-sized millerighe.

Olive oil There is no doubt that extra-virgin olive oil has more flavour than refined olive oil; both are equally beneficial, however. I use refined olive oil for general cooking and reserve extra-virgin olive oil for salad dressings and special pasta dressings where the flavour of the oil is particularly important.

Orecchiette (little ears) Home-made pasta from Puglia, similar to cavatieddi but shaped like tiny priests' hats. Happily, they are now manufactured and available outside Italy, and are perfect with vegetable sauces.

Pancetta *Pancetta* or belly pork is chopped finely and used as a basic fat ingredient in many Italian dishes. Although it is readily available I prefer to use bacon as it is leaner.

Pappardelle Wide tagliatelle favoured in Tuscany, best served with a game or rich meat ragù.

Pasta al forno All pasta dishes finished in the oven come under this heading. Be sure to boil the pasta for less than the recommended time as it continues cooking in the heat of the oven.

Pasta all'uovo Egg pasta, either manufactured or hand-made (tagliatelle, lasagne, cannelloni etc.).

Pasta asciutta Any pasta, dried or fresh, served in a sauce rather than in a soup or broth.

Pasta corta Manufactured dried pasta shapes (penne, millerighe, tortiglioni etc.) made from semolina flour.

Pasta farcita Stuffed pasta (tortellini, tortelloni, ravioli etc.).

Pasta fresca Fresh pasta; the ingredients vary from region to region but it is generally made from plain flour and eggs.

Pasta lunga Long shapes of manufactured pasta, made from semolina flour (spaghetti, capellini, fidelini, spaghettoni, bucatini, etc.).

Pasta piccola Tiny pasta shapes added to broth, consommé and soups (sambucca flowers, partridge eyes, little squares, little rings, etc.).

Pastella Light, coating batter.

Pasticcio A large shortcrust parcel from Emilia filled with layers of pasta, tagliatelle, maccheroni or tortellini dressed with béchamel sauce and a rich ragù.

Penne (quills) Ridged or smooth maccheroni 3 cm (1¼ in) long, cut on the slant at both ends like a quill pen.

Polenta Bright yellow 'pudding' made from maize flour and boiling water stirred over heat with a stick for an hour until thick and smooth like porridge. It is then turned on to a cloth, cut into slices and served with a rich meat, fish or game sauce (see page 22 for the basic polenta recipe).

Ravioli Squares of filled pasta, also known as pansooti and tortelli.

Rigatoni Large, fat, ridged maccheroni, excellent with meat and tomato sauce. Denti d'elefante (elephant's teeth) are similar but narrower; sedanini (little celeries) are narrower still.

Sfoglia The sheet of hand-rolled pasta from which all egg pasta shapes are cut.

Spaghetti, spaghettini, spaghettoni Spaghetti-type pastas come in varying thicknesses, and each manufacturer produces more than one size. Spaghettini are the most popular in Italy but are not always readily available elsewhere.

Tagliatelle (small cuts) The name commonly given to 1 cm (½ in) ribbons of *pasta all'uovo*; tagliolini are half that width. The g is silent – talyatellay.

Timballo Generally used for pasta or rice tossed in a sauce, pressed into a breadcrumbed mould and turned out. Also known as a *sformato*.

Tomatoes Serving spaghetti with tomato sauce was a Neapolitan invention of the nineteenth century. It soon became popular with the masses and was adopted by every Italian region. There are many ways of preparing the sauce (see pages 23–24).

Canned tomatoes make an excellent substitute for fresh plum tomatoes. A tomato-based sauce should be creamy rather than sloppy. To achieve this always strain the juice from the tomatoes and set on one side. Cut open the tomatoes, discard the seeds and cut the flesh into strips. Reserve the tomato juice to use as stock.

In recent years sun-dried tomatoes have become popular and today can be found on most delicatessen shelves. They are traditionally a product of southern Italy, where tomatoes are preserved through the winter by drying in the sun rather than making *conserva*.

Tortellini Tiny, ring-shaped parcels of egg pasta containing a mixture of fresh meat, cured meat and parmesan cheese; originally from Bologna. They are also known as agnolini, anolini and cappelletti.

Tortelloni Twists of egg pasta, traditionally filled with flavoured ricotta; lobster, salmon, chicken, white fish or vegetable stuffings can also be used. A speciality of Bologna, where they are also known as agnolotti.

Tortiglioni Short lengths of twisted ridged maccheroni.

Trenette Narrow tagliatelle, favoured in Liguria.

Trito See **Battuto**.

Vermicelli The name used in the south and in Sicily for fine spaghetti.

Zite Long strands of smooth, straight maccheroni, favoured in southern Italy.

SELECT BIBLIOGRAPHY

Italian Food, Elizabeth David, Harmondsworth 1974.

La Scienza in Cucina e l'Arte di Mangiar Bene, Pellegrino Artusi, Torino 1970.

Le Ricette Regionali Italiane, Anna Gosetti della Salda, Milano 1977.

La Pasta Asciutta, Ripiena, al Forno, Luigi Carnacina, Milano 1976.

Ricette Traditionali della Liguria, Lucetto Ramella, Imperia 1978.

Il Talismano della Felicità, Ada Boni, Roma 1991.

Dictionary of Gastronomy, André L. Simon and Robin Howe, London 1978.

Culpeper's Complete Herbal, Nicholas Culpeper, Ware 1985.

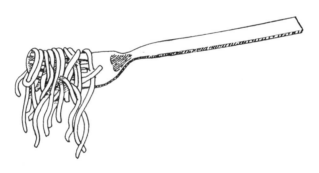

INDEX